Meditations after Holy Communion

Fr. Edward Looney

Meditations after Holy Communion
Guided Meditations for Every Sunday and Other Holy Days

SOPHIA INSTITUTE PRESS

Manchester, New Hampshire

Sophia Institute Press
Box 5284, Manchester, NH 03108
1-800-888-9344

www.SophiaInstitute.com

Sophia Institute Press® is a registered trademark of Sophia Institute.

paperback ISBN 978-1-64413-344-6

ebook ISBN 978-1-64413-345-3

Library of Congress Control Number: 2020946007

First printing

*In gratitude to those who taught me the
importance of the Holy Eucharist throughout my life,
especially my First Communion catechist, Sr. Lipharda;
the priest who administered my
First Holy Communion, Fr. Bob Groher;
all the faithful with whom I attended Mass
as a member of the congregation;
and those for whom I now celebrate Mass each day.
Your devotion and commitment to the Eucharist
have inspired me.*

Contents

Ordinary Time

Other Holy Days

Introduction

We live in a time in the Church when, statistically, the majority of Catholics do not believe in the Real Presence of Jesus in the Eucharist. Some mistakenly believe that the Eucharist is only a symbol. Perhaps the genesis of this crisis of belief comes out of our approach to the sacraments. Maybe it has to do with our preparation and what happens during and after our reception of the Holy Eucharist.

"Truly it is You!" This is a prayer that I say during every Mass, following the Consecration of the bread and wine into the Body, Blood, Soul, and Divinity of our Savior, Jesus Christ. I started praying this prayer because, as a new priest, I wanted to reaffirm that what I celebrated was real. I found myself saying three to five Masses on any given weekend, and by the time I reached the third or fourth Mass, I felt I was becoming numb to the mystery I was celebrating. I lacked awe and wonder at the God made flesh present on the altar. That prayer, "Truly it is You," became a reminder to me that what I was celebrating was real, that Jesus' words at the Last Supper change reality: bread and wine remain no more, having become the Body and Blood of Christ.

I remember, as a young boy, entering our parish church for Sunday Mass, kneeling after entering the pew, and saying a few short prayers. Now, as a priest, I am amazed by the countless faithful who do that same ritual I did in my youth. Today, because of our busy schedules, it's possible that there is no time for silent prayer before Mass. Maybe you are lucky if you get there in time for the opening song. But if you do arrive early, what do you do in those moments before Mass begins? Maybe it is a simple exchange with God about what is weighing most on your heart or mind. Or there might be a prayer you usually recite before Mass.

After I received my driver's license, I would occasionally drive to Green Bay to attend the Extraordinary Form of the Mass. I had a friend whose family went to that form of the Mass, and I would go to experience it and to spend time with them. Two things struck me about those experiences. The first was the reliance on the missal to get me through the Mass. The book contained side-by-side Latin and English, so I could follow the Mass. But it also had recommended prayers before Mass, before Communion, after Communion, and after Mass. Before going to the Extraordinary Form, I was aware of only one such prayer, the Anima Christi. The missal introduced me to others from saints such as Thomas Aquinas and Bonaventure.

The second thing that struck me was what happened after Mass. The church did not erupt into conversation. Instead, everyone knelt afterward and said prayers of gratitude. As I looked around, everyone was using missals to assist them in their prayer. It made sense to do that. If we receive the Body and Blood of Jesus at Mass, and those moments after Holy Communion are so special, it makes sense for us to spend time in prayerful dialogue and thanksgiving to Jesus for the gift we received.

When I went to the seminary, I noticed that some, but not all, would do a similar thing. At the conclusion of Mass, some would kneel and others would leave. I imagine that everyone made some sort of thanksgiving, and the reality is, it could happen in those moments immediately following Holy Communion. Since I was very young, I always had one prayer I would say after receiving the Eucharist: the Anima Christi. I happened upon the prayer in a prayer book along with the words "Indulgence 300 Days." I didn't know what that meant, but as young boy, I concluded it meant I had to pray the prayer for 300 days. I later was taught that the language meant "time off" from Purgatory or was equivalent of doing 300 days of penance. The antiquated language of days was abrogated by Pope Paul VI's 1968 *Enchiridion Indulgentiarum* for several reasons. First, because it was confusing. Secondly, because there is no time in eternity. God is outside of time because, to Him, a thousand years seem like only one day (Ps. 90:4). With indulgences, we leave it up to God to determine its outcome for each soul. This antiquated language with indulgences is no longer used, but the text meant at one time that when you prayed that prayer, you would receive an indulgence lessening your stay in Purgatory by three hundred days. I think you can see why we no longer use this language! Being young, I mistook that information as signifying that I had to pray the prayer after Holy Communion for three hundred days, meaning it could take me close to six years! I even started to keep track of those days. I'm sure by now I have surpassed the three hundred days many times over, but it remains a prayer I say when I return to the presider's chair after the purification of the vessels during Mass. Many of the faithful will have had time to commune with God during the song and the purification, but I prolong the silence for just a few more seconds so I can say this prayer.

In the seminary, when my fellow seminarians would make their thanksgiving, most did not hold a book in their hands as I had seen done at the Latin Mass. Most likely they prayed from their heart or engaged in meditation on their own. But for someone just starting out with Eucharistic thanksgivings and meditations, where might they start? Who teaches them what to do in those moments? I would discover the answer a few years into my priesthood.

In October of 2016, I found myself in a theological library. I hoped to discover something that would help me come up with a paper topic for an academic conference on Mariology. My initial idea was to examine those old missals people used during the Latin Mass and look for prayers for after Communion or after Mass that reference the Blessed Mother. I hoped to discover some theology related to Mary, the Eucharist, and ourselves, and to explicate said theology in the presentation of my paper. As I had suspected, when I searched the missals, I found prayers referencing Mary as a tabernacle and a monstrance and a recipient of Christ. In my continued search, I looked at the shelf behind me, which contained devotional literature, and a title caught my eye: *Christ in Me*. I picked the book off the shelf, thinking that, because Mary had Christ in her, perhaps this book referenced her. The subtitle of the book was exactly what I was looking for: *Meditations after Holy Communion*. The book was written by a Jesuit, Fr. Daniel Lord, who was a prolific writer in the first half of the 1900s. I consulted the table of contents and discovered that there were twelve meditations focused on Mary's relationship to the Eucharist.

It seems that God always sends me the spiritual writer I need at a particular time: this book was what I craved — to delve deeper into the Eucharistic mystery. I wanted to know how I should meditate after Mass or after receiving Holy Communion. I prayed with the meditations, and Fr. Lord taught me how to make a Eucharistic thanksgiving or meditation. Not only that, but Fr.

4

Lord's meditations became the basis of my paper presentation, "Theological Themes in the Marian Eucharistic Meditations of Fr. Daniel A. Lord." After I delivered the paper, a fellow scholar approached me and encouraged me to write a book to teach people how to make a prayerful meditation and thanksgiving after Holy Communion or Mass. As you hold this book in your hands, you can see that her suggestion has come to fruition.

Two of the books I have written have come from my spiritual life. In *A Rosary Litany*, I renewed a method of praying the Rosary taught by St. Louis de Montfort that I accidentally discovered and then began using in my life. I found it beneficial and wished to share it with others. *A Heart Like Mary's* came from my spiritual director's challenging words, asking me, "Where is your Marian heart?" That question led me to reflect at great length on what it means to have a Marian heart. Now, *Meditations after Holy Communion* comes from my own meditation topics following Mass.

I hope that this book will become an entry point to a lifelong habit of dialogue with our Lord following your reception of Holy Communion, when He comes to dwell under your roof. My aim in this book is to provide you with topics to meditate on. After introducing each meditation, I explain how you can engage it for a few moments of quiet prayer and reflection, and then I close with a short prayer capitulating the topic of the week.

In the introduction to *Christ in Me*, Fr. Lord told his readers that he hoped they wouldn't need his book and would never read it. In other words, the meditations he wrote are meant to serve as a guide and be a pedagogical tool, helping a person to meditate following Holy Communion. Fr. Lord wrote his meditations in several segments that people could read, but he encouraged his readers to put the book down and reflect on only one of his points at a time. His hope was that by the time his readers finished his book, they would be equipped to meditate on their own without the help of a book.

As I share my meditative thoughts with you, I hope they will teach you how to make a prayerful meditation and that once you make your way through this book, you will no longer require this aid and can give it to someone else, so that that person can deepen his or her relationship with our Eucharistic Lord. The book contains meditations for every Sunday and for holy days and other significant feast days, with the idea that you can use it each week as you attend Mass, thus using it for an entire year. If you are a daily communicant and wish to use the weekly meditations daily, the book will guide you through about two months of Masses.

Truly Christ is present in the Eucharist, present in all the tabernacles of the world. But He is also present in us each time we receive Him. And just as we speak to Christ reserved in the tabernacle or the monstrance, we can speak to Him in those intimate moments following Holy Communion. I hope, like me, you will be able to acclaim at every Mass, "Truly it is You!"

How to Use This Book

The concept of this book is straightforward: it is a book of meditations to be used each Sunday and for special liturgical celebrations throughout the year. Each meditation has a preface that sets the scene and gives you something to think about. It then moves into points to ponder and a short prayer. How you use the book is up to you. Initially, I thought that it would be best to read the preface after Holy Communion or Mass and engage the prayerful meditations for about five minutes. This would be one good practice.

As I continued to write the book and talk about it with others, another idea came to me. You could read the preface of the meditation before attending Mass and then, after Communion or Mass, you could converse with Jesus about the "Points to Ponder" and close with the day's prayer.

I even began envisioning that this book could be used for family prayer associated with Mass. I imagined that a family could read the preface together in the car before Mass and then have a conversation on the way home about one of the "Points to Ponder." Not all the points would be good for group conversation because some are of a more personal nature, but each day has some points that would be conducive to group sharing. It is helpful for us to talk about our spiritual lives with our families and to share with them how God is acting in our lives.

However you decide to use this book, I hope that it will be for your spiritual edification and that it will teach you to converse with Jesus in those special moments after receiving Him in Holy Communion.

Advent and Christmas

First Sunday of Advent

I Wait for the Lord

———— ❀ ————

From the Fall of man to the first Christmas morning, the world waited with longing and expectation for the coming of the Messiah, who would save us from our sins. Many figures of the Old Testament, such as Noah and Moses, prefigured or pointed to Jesus, which is why we call Him the "New Noah" or the "New Moses." The prophets spoke of the coming Messiah years before He came. Mary, the Virgin Mother, we hear in Preface II of Advent, "longed for Him with love beyond all telling."

Advent is a time of waiting. Sometimes in our world, this waiting is difficult. In fact, already in these early days of Advent, people are celebrating Christmas with music and parties. Now, at the beginning of Advent, make a resolution to slow down and, with the people of long ago, wait for the Lord.

Points to Ponder

What do you do when you wait? Do you look at your phone and scroll through social media? Are you comfortable with silence?

Meditations after Holy Communion

What was it like for Mary to be with child
and to wait to see the One foretold by the
prophets and announced by an angel?

*Lord Jesus, all through Mass, I wait for the intimate
moment when I receive You in Holy Communion. Let
my heart and my entire body long for Your coming — in
the Eucharist, on Christmas Day, and at the end of
time.*

Second Sunday of Advent

Prepare the Way of the Lord

One of the central figures of the Advent season is John the Baptist. He is the one the archangel Gabriel was speaking about when he told Mary that her cousin, who was barren and advanced in years, was with child and in her sixth month. The Gospels tell us that John the Baptist was a voice crying out in the desert to prepare the way of the Lord (see Matt. 3:3; Mark 1:3; Luke 3:4; John 1:23). We often think of Lent as an intentional season of preparation with prayer, penance, and almsgiving. Advent is a time of preparation too. We prepare our homes for celebrations. We prepare by shopping for gifts and writing Christmas cards. How do we prepare spiritually for Christmas? Some recommendations include celebrating the sacrament of Reconciliation, praying the Rosary or the Angelus or some other form of prayer, and reading the Gospels. If you choose to slow down just a little and engage the spiritual life each day, when Christmas Day comes, although you might feel exhausted from all the running around you have done, you will have greater peace. Listen to St. John the Baptist and prepare your heart and soul for the Lord's coming.

Meditations after Holy Communion

Points to Ponder

What is it that you need to do to prepare yourself for
Christmas? How have you been preparing? Where
have you failed? What could you be doing better?

*Lord Jesus, I need Your help each day to prepare for
Your coming. Give me wisdom so I will be prepared
for Christmas, each Eucharistic encounter, and Your
appearance at the end of my life.*

Third Sunday of Advent

Rejoice!

This Sunday has a special moniker: Gaudete Sunday. *Gaudete* is a Latin word that means "rejoice." The priest has the option to wear a rose vestment for Mass today instead of the purple one he has been wearing during Advent. We rejoice today because the day of our salvation draws near, when Mary brings forth Christ our Lord. We rejoice because soon Heaven will meet earth. At each Mass we attend, Heaven meets earth, because Jesus becomes present in the Holy Eucharist on the altar. Just as we have joy because Christmas is approaching, we should be filled with joy every time we approach the altar because of that privileged encounter we have with our Eucharistic Lord. It's okay if we don't experience it every time, but it is something for which we should pray and strive.

Points to Ponder

What is your disposition today? Are you happy? Sad? Angry? If you do not feel happy or joyful, why is that? Is there anything you can do to change that? Who can help you?

Meditations after Holy Communion

What things bring you joy and happiness?
Thank God for those people or things.

When you receive Holy Communion, are you
overcome with a sense of joy? If not, ask God
for the grace of joy each time you receive.

*Lord Jesus, I ask You to take away anything that strips
me of joy. I want to experience life as You want me
to—filled with joy and gladness. Help me to rejoice in
all circumstances, especially when I receive Your Body
and Blood in Holy Communion.*

I Carry Christ with Me

I once heard a preacher say that Mary was the first Eucharistic procession. Why? Because when she set out in haste to visit her cousin Elizabeth, she carried the Word made flesh in her womb. Mary was a living tabernacle. John the Baptist acknowledges Christ's presence in Mary's womb by leaping for joy in his mother's womb. Wherever Mary went during those nine months of pregnancy, Christ went with her. Mary brought Jesus to people, whether they knew it or not. That's something to sit with for a few moments: all the people who were touched by grace, in the presence of God, without even knowing it. Then Mary went home to Nazareth, only to pick up and go to Bethlehem, where she would give birth.

Points to Ponder

Where are you going today? Whom will you visit? What is on your agenda this week? Will you go to a child's or a grandchild's sporting event? When you go, will people know you are a Christian? Wherever you go, how can you intentionally bring Christ to whomever you meet?

Meditations after Holy Communion

Lord Jesus, in these moments after Holy Communion, You live inside me. As I go forward from Mass, I carry You with me. Please do not depart from me. Be with me through all my encounters and experiences of today, tomorrow, and the rest of the week. Make me a fitting tabernacle of Your presence and a traveling monstrance of Your love and mercy.

Christmas

House of Bread

━━━━━━━━━ ❀ ━━━━━━━━━

"O little town of Bethlehem, how still we see thee lie." In the Christmas story, this small city in Israel (today Palestine) has a central role. It is the town where the Son of God was born of the Virgin Mary.

The name Bethlehem means "house of bread." Isn't it interesting that the Son of God, who would later tell us that He is the Bread of Life, the Bread come down from Heaven, who would give His Body and Blood to the disciples at the Last Supper, was born in a village whose name means "house of bread"?

In every church, there is a small house of bread called a tabernacle, where the God of the universe resides, waiting to be adored and loved. In one sense, we have all become a little Bethlehem because God enters under our roofs, as we pray at Mass. That "house" refers to our body, and through our reception of Holy Communion, we, too, have become a home for the supernatural bread that is Jesus Christ.

Meditations after Holy Communion

Points to Ponder

Use your imagination or look at the nativity scene
at your parish and allow that to enlighten your
imagination. Picture the scene: Mary and Joseph
there, the shepherds and the Magi—all of these
Christmas figures adoring Christ the Lord. Can you
simply sit there and adore the Christ Child with His
mother, His foster father, and the other onlookers?
In your imagination, ask Mary if you can hold the
Christ Child. Do you kiss the Child's head?

*Thank You, Lord, for being born in Bethlehem for us.
By becoming the Word made flesh, You began Your work
of redemption. Thank You for the gift of the Eucharist
and for allowing me to become a little Bethlehem.*

The Holy Family

Praying for Your Family

Fr. Patrick Peyton, C.S.C., was known for his phrase "The family that prays together stays together." Maybe you are at Mass today because, when you were growing up, your family made Sunday Eucharist a priority and that is something that has stayed with you throughout your life. In your childhood, you sat in a pew in your church with your family at your side. Maybe you have some memories of those experiences or the scolding you received when you misbehaved. As you grew in age and formed your own family, the cycle repeated itself, and hopefully you have handed on to your children the importance of Sunday Mass.

What happens at the parish church should also be reflected in the home. That is why we call the home the domestic church. At Mass, we ask for forgiveness, we hear the Word of God, we reflect, we pray, and we share a meal. In your domestic church, tell each other you are sorry for any offenses you have committed, read the Scriptures and share some thoughts, pray for those in need, and sit down at the dinner table and share a meal. On this feast of the Holy Family, give some thought to how you can pray together as a family and how you can pray for your family.

Meditations after Holy Communion

Points to Ponder

What was your experience of Sunday Mass
like when you were growing up? How have you
promoted Sunday Mass with your own family?

When you are at Mass, do you pray for your family?
Who in your family needs prayers the most right now?

What part of your Sunday experience can you
replicate this week in your domestic church?

*Lord Jesus, through the Eucharist, You unite my family,
for we share communion together with You. Thank You
for the family I was born into and the way they blessed
me as a child. I pray for my own family now, that You
will grant them happiness, health, and well-being. Help
us to live and love together, so that one day we may be
united together in the Kingdom of Heaven.*

Mary, Mother of God (January 1)

Mary Treasured in Her Heart

Holy days offer us opportunities to make holy our daily lives. If we are committed, they compel us to attend Holy Mass, not because it is an obligation but because it is an opportunity. January 1, New Year's Day, might seem like an inconvenient day to go to Mass. Perhaps it is because we celebrated the night before and there is not a convenient Mass time. But how blessed we are to celebrate the New Year by asking Mary's prayers and receiving the Eucharist! When I was in college, a local parish offered a Holy Hour as a way to end the year and a midnight Mass as a way to begin the year with the Eucharist.

One of the most beautiful aspects of Mary's example in Scripture is that she treasured the moments of Jesus' life in her heart, as St. Luke repeats (2:19, 51). Think of all the memories of Jesus that Mary had: His first words; His first steps; all the things He did in His childhood. Like Mary, we can treasure the special moments of our lives. At the beginning of this new year, spend a few moments treasuring the moments of the past year, and when you do so, you will be imitating the Blessed Virgin.

Meditations after Holy Communion

Points to Ponder

How did Mary treasure and ponder? What
part of her life with Jesus do you want to think
about and dwell on for a few moments?

What are some of your fondest memories for
which you are grateful? What is something
you treasure from the last year?

*Lord Jesus, I remember most especially every Holy
Communion I received this past year, and I am grateful
for this gift of union with You. Help me, united with
Mary, to treasure, as she did, all the graces and
blessings of my life.*

Epiphany

My Gift for Jesus

———— ✦ ————

The feast of Epiphany recalls the visit of the Magi to Jesus. The Magi brought gold, frankincense, and myrrh, but surely they were not the only people who brought gifts for the newborn King and His family. Many nativity scenes show several other characters. Maybe someone brought the gift of a meal. We remember that the little drummer had no gift to bring that was fit for a king, so he played his drum; he himself became a gift for the Lord. What can we offer the Lord today? We can bring Him our adoration and worship. We can offer Him our praise and thanksgiving. We can bring Him our good works and virtuous living. There is some gift we can bring Jesus today. We just need to name it and give it to Him.

Points to Ponder

What are some gifts that you think Jesus received
that are not known to us? What are gifts that you
have given to the Lord? What will your gift for
Him be today? What gifts has Jesus given you?

Meditations after Holy Communion

Lord Jesus, I receive the greatest gift every time I receive you in Holy Communion. On this day, when Your family received the gifts of the Magi, I wish to offer You a gift, the gift of my love and service. I love You, Lord; I praise and adore You. Receive my gift and be pleased with it this day.

The Baptism of the Lord

Be Well Pleased with Me

At the beginning of every Mass, we are invited to pause and call to mind our sins, asking the Lord's mercy and pardon. And then we say at least one of three prayers: the Confiteor, the Kyrie, or "Have mercy on us, O Lord." In these prayers, we acknowledge before God that we are unworthy, that we have failed, and that we need His mercy and forgiveness.

On the feast of the Baptism of the Lord, we hear God the Father say, "This is my beloved Son, with whom I am well pleased" (Matt. 3:17). There are probably some things we have done in our lives that have not been pleasing to God. Consequently, we received the sacrament of Reconciliation and asked God for forgiveness. Through the celebration of that sacrament, we resolved to sin no more and to avoid the near occasion of sin, meaning that we wanted to please God with our words and our conduct. When we come to Mass, we examine our consciences and ask ourselves, "How have I lived a life pleasing to the Lord?" With our reception of Holy Communion today, let us ask the Lord to increase in us the desire to live lives pleasing to Him.

Meditations after Holy Communion

Points to Ponder

At Mass, when you are invited by the priest to pause and call to mind your sins, do you? Have you committed any sins in the previous week?

In your everyday life, do you ask yourself, "Is the Lord pleased with this?" What actions do you need to take to live a life more pleasing to the Lord? How do you live the grace of your Baptism?

Lord Jesus, I am sorry for the times I offended You by my words and actions. As I hear the Father say that He is well pleased with You, I want Him to say that about me too. Through the grace of the Holy Eucharist I received, help me to live a life faithful to You and Your commandments.

Lent and Easter

Ash Wednesday

Hungering for the Lord

—————⊛—————

Ash Wednesday and Good Friday are two unique days of the year, because the Church asks us to fast on those days. The fasting regulations allow one full meal and two smaller meals that do not equate to the full meal. Some people might do a stricter fast — for example, bread and water alone. On fast days, when we eat less, we begin to notice the feeling of hunger. On a day of penitence, that hunger signals our longing for God.

Throughout the year, whenever we attend Mass, the Church expects us to fast for one hour before our reception of Holy Communion. Although this might mean denying ourselves some food or snack, we should realize that we do so because we are going to feast on something greater.

Points to Ponder

Think about all those who are hungry in the
world today — not only physically hungry but
spiritually hungry. Those who are spiritually

Meditations after Holy Communion

hungry have separated themselves from God
and try to fill that hunger with other things.

Have you experienced spiritual hunger before? Do you
observe the one-hour fast before Holy Communion?

There are stories of individuals who lived on the
Eucharist alone for long periods. Give some thought
to that reality—of living on Christ alone.

*Thank You, Jesus, for feeding me with the Eucharist
and fulfilling the longing I have for You. Give me a
hunger for You week after week so I will always return
to your Eucharistic banquet.*

First Sunday of Lent

Overcoming Temptation

-----------------◈-----------------

At every Mass, we pray the Our Father, the prayer Jesus taught His disciples when they asked Him to teach them how to pray. You might say the Our Father many times a day—six times in the Rosary and twice if you pray Morning and Evening Prayer from the Liturgy of the Hours. We know the prayer so well that we can race through it. Fr. Larry Richards leads the Our Father slowly at every Mass so the faithful can focus on the words. When I go to Confession, my penance is sometimes to pray the Our Father slowly and think about the meaning of each word.

One of the phrases we pray in the Our Father is "lead us not into temptation." In our daily lives, we are faced with decisions to do right or wrong, to tell the truth or to lie, to say kind things or to gossip. As you go about your week, notice how often you are tempted. Become aware of those moments. Pray for God's strength. And remain faithful to the Lord. In the Gospel for the First Sunday of Lent, Satan tempts Jesus, but Jesus withstands each temptation. Let us try to resist like Jesus and conquer evil by His power.

Meditations after Holy Communion

Points to Ponder

What is the greatest temptation you face on a daily basis? Is there a particular sin that you have overcome? How did you claim victory? What are some spiritual tools that are available to you that can help you confront the temptations you face daily?

Lord Jesus, by the Eucharist I have received, strengthen me to overcome sin, to resist temptation, and always to remain faithful to Your commands.

Second Sunday of Lent

Remaining with the Lord

Every second Sunday of Lent, we hear the Gospel of the Transfiguration—that experience of the three apostles who ascend Mount Tabor with Jesus and see Him become radiant and hear Him converse with Moses and Elijah. Afterward, they hear a voice from Heaven say, "This is my beloved Son . . . ; listen to him" (Matt. 17:5). During the experience, Peter says to Jesus, "Lord, it is well that we are here; if you wish, I will make three booths here, one for you and one for Moses and one for Elijah" (Matt. 17:4). St. Peter expresses his desire to remain with the Lord in that moment. He is so caught up that he doesn't want to leave.

That should be our experience at every Mass: like Peter, we should be so happy that we want to remain in the church and spend time with the Lord. At the Consecration, when the priest elevates the Host for a few moments of adoration, we should yearn to have just a few more moments of adoration. You might have noticed that desire to remain with the Lord. It is possible for that desire to be fulfilled: many churches offer adoration, whether it is for an hour every so often, daily, or even perpetual. Even if adoration is not available, we know that Jesus is present in the tabernacle and we can stop by any open church and pray before the reposed Blessed Sacrament. This is the beautiful thing about Jesus: He wants to fulfill the desires and longings of our hearts. If we want to remain with Him, He offers us opportunities; we just need to make ourselves available to Him.

Points to Ponder

Recall a time in your life (it doesn't have to be a religious experience) when you didn't want a certain moment to pass and you simply wanted to remain in that moment forever. What did you experience? Why was it so moving? Have you had any religious experiences like that?

Do you ever want to remain with Jesus in church for longer than you are able?

What is the deepest desire of your heart right now?

Jesus, thank You for allowing me to receive You in Holy Communion. I wish to remain in this moment, knowing how close You are to me.

What Does Jesus Know about You?

Jesus went to a Samaritan village, where He met a woman who was drawing water from the well. It went against social norms for Jesus to talk to the woman, but He did anyway. In His conversation with her, He told her things that no one else knew about her. We see this elsewhere in the Gospels, where Jesus knew the hearts of people and what they were thinking. He is the God of the universe; He knows everything! The Samaritan woman went into the village afterward and told people that she had met a man who knew everything about her. The reality is that Jesus knows everything about us too.

When it comes to knowledge, there are things that you know about yourself and everybody else knows too. Then there are things that you know, but nobody else knows, because you haven't shared those things. And there are things that others might know about you that you might not know, such as your quirks or shortcomings. Spiritually speaking, God knows things about us that we don't know about ourselves. He knows our every hurt and our every wound. He is our Creator, and He knows the number of hairs on our heads and when we sit or stand (see Matt. 10:30; Ps.

139:2). Just as Jesus revealed to that woman at the well so many things about her life, if we ask Him, He will do the same for us.

Points to Ponder

What are some things that everybody knows about you? What are the things you have hidden from other people? Why? Ask Jesus to reveal to you the things you don't know about yourself so that you might bring them to Him for healing.

Jesus, I know that you listen to me when I share the heaviness of my heart. Help me to listen to Your inner stirrings in my soul so that I might know You and myself more.

"Lord, I Believe"

There was a man blind from birth who sat by the Pool of Siloam. One day, Jesus saw this blind man and was moved to compassion for him. Jesus made a healing balm and applied it to the man's eyes. Eventually the man was able to see. The man was subjected to many questions about who had healed him, and he was ostracized after giving his testimony. Jesus heard what happened to the man and went and found him and asked him, "Do you believe in the Son of man?" After a brief exchange with Jesus, the healed man exclaimed, "Lord, I believe" (John 9:35, 38).

Every Sunday we are asked a similar question: "Do you believe?" Everything we do at Mass revolves around faith. When we acknowledge our sins and ask for mercy at the beginning of Mass, we have to have faith that God forgives our venial sins. When we hear the Scripture readings proclaimed, we have to have faith that what the author wrote is true. We profess an entire creed of statements about who God is, and we say "I believe" in each of those statements. When we pray, "Lord, hear our prayer," we have to believe that He hears the prayers we offer. And especially when we hear the words of consecration and present ourselves for Holy Communion and hear the words "The Body of Christ," we say with our entire body, "Amen," which means, "Lord, I believe." If we have doubts, we must ask Jesus to give us a deeper faith in these mysteries.

Points to Ponder

What do you believe? Do you believe that Jesus forgives your sins? Do you believe all the things you hear about in Sacred Scripture, or do you approach anything with skepticism? When you professed the Creed at Mass today, were there some statements you didn't understand or had difficulty believing?

How do you approach prayer?

Do you believe that the Host you receive in Holy Communion is Jesus?

Jesus, I believe that You are who You say You are. I believe You are present in the Holy Eucharist. When I am unbelieving, help me to believe.

Fifth Sunday of Lent

Tell or Ask Jesus Anything

When people encountered Jesus while He lived on earth, they asked Him questions. After all, He is the God of the universe and is all-knowing. He was a great teacher, so many people drew close to Him to hear His inspired words of teaching and preaching. Martha and Mary and their brother Lazarus were friends of Jesus. Jesus wept over Lazarus's death. But He knew that He would summon Lazarus forth from the tomb.

Mary came to Jesus and said to Him, "Lord, if you had been here, my brother would not have died" (John 11:32). She spoke to Jesus from a place of grief. She related to Him how she felt and put it all out there. The Gospels tell of other people who asked Jesus questions too. A rich man asked Him, "What must I do to inherit eternal life?" What these people in the Gospels did is something we can do today and, to be honest, every day of our lives, through our prayer.

At times in my life, I have asked Jesus, "Why did this have to happen?" or "What do You want me to do?" or I tell Him, "I just don't get it." Give yourself permission to be honest with Jesus today. If something is bothering you, share it with Him. If you are angry, tell Him. If you ask or tell Jesus whatever is on your mind or heart, you will have a greater sense of peace and you might even receive some direction from Him.

Points to Ponder

When was the last real conversation you had
with Jesus? Do you regularly share with Him
your thoughts, feelings, desires, and struggles?
What do you want to tell Him today?

Jesus, You are with me, and I wish to talk to You as my friend. I need Your help. I need guidance. I need a shoulder to rest my head on. I need someone to listen to me. I know that is what You want to do for me. I come to You now as one who has labored, and I am seeking the rest You offer.

Palm Sunday

Jesus, Save Us!

Palm Sunday begins with Jesus' triumphal entry into Jerusalem, riding on a donkey. People greet Him by laying palm branches on the ground, and the sound of hosannas can be heard. The word "hosanna" is one we sing or say at every Mass in the Sanctus, or the Holy, Holy, Holy. We sing, "Hosanna in the highest." Have you ever paused to think about what "hosanna" means? It's a Hebrew word that means "save us," "deliver us," or "rescue us." As we begin the celebration of Holy Week, we recall that that is exactly what Jesus intends to do. He will take upon Himself the sins of all humankind and become the sacrificial offering. The sin offerings of the past will no longer be necessary because Jesus will save us from our sins.

Maybe there has been a time in your life when you had to cry out, "Save me!" I remember when I fell off a dock into a river, and I was frantic because it all happened so fast. Someone jumped into the water and helped me get to safety. I know that I am in need of a savior for my many faults and sins. When I feel helpless, I need Jesus to save me. When I am overwhelmed by emotions, I need to call out to Jesus and ask Him to save me. And every Sunday when we sing "hosanna," we make that petition known to Jesus, asking Him to save us in the ways He knows we need saving.

Points to Ponder

Has any person in your life been there to save you from something devastating? Maybe a parent, a friend, a neighbor, or even a stranger? Have you reached out and helped another person in a crisis moment?

Can you recall a moment when you cried out to God with the words "Save me" or "Help me"?

Jesus, by the power of the Eucharist I receive, I know that You save me and help me. In my most difficult and desperate moments, I ask You to rescue me. Thank You for Your grace.

Holy Thursday

The Apostles' First Communion

Jesus and the apostles were Jewish and celebrated the feasts of the Jewish people. This means that they celebrated Passover. At Mass on Holy Thursday, we hear the account of the Passover meal from the book of Exodus and hear how it is to be eaten.

In the Upper Room, on the night of the Last Supper, this is the meal Jesus sat down to share with His followers. Just as the God of Abraham, Isaac, and Jacob made a covenant with the Jewish people, Jesus instituted a new covenant that night, by taking bread and wine and saying the words "This is my body," "This is my blood." He then commanded the apostles to continue gathering at table and doing what He did in remembrance of Him. After saying those words, Jesus broke the bread and gave it to His disciples, and they received their First Holy Communion. On Holy Thursday, that is precisely what we do, gathering in the church to celebrate the institution of the Holy Eucharist.

Meditations after Holy Communion

Points to Ponder

What do you think the apostles thought when Jesus took bread and wine and said those words for the first time? Do you think they recalled the words of Jesus in John, chapter 6: "He who eats my flesh and drinks my blood has eternal life" (John 6:54)? How do you think the apostles felt after they received the Eucharist for the first time? Did they feel calmness and peace?

How do you feel after you receive?

Lord Jesus, fill me with the same awe that filled Your apostles on the night of the Last Supper. Let every Holy Communion I receive be as if it were my first.

Good Friday

The Day with No Mass

Good Friday is such a peculiar day, especially in the Church. On this day, there is no public celebration of the Eucharist. But in the Good Friday liturgy, we do have an opportunity to receive Holy Communion, which was consecrated during Holy Thursday Mass. You might wonder why there is no Mass that day. As Catholics, we believe that the celebration of Mass is a representation of Calvary, because Jesus offers Himself as the sacrifice for sins. Sometimes the Mass is called the "holy sacrifice of the Mass" for this very reason. On Good Friday, when that sacrifice and death on the Cross is so central, the Church believes there is no need to offer the sacrifice of the Mass and that not having the Consecration emphasizes the Church's sense of loss over Jesus' death. On the night of the Last Supper, we heard Jesus say those words, "This is my body.... This is my blood." On Good Friday, looking at a crucifix, we behold the body and blood of the Savior—a body that is broken and bleeding.

What is missing on Good Friday? The offering of the bread and wine, the Preface, and the Eucharistic prayer. Instead, the Word of God is proclaimed, the solemn petitions are offered, and veneration of the crucifix takes place before the opportunity to receive Holy Communion. Even though we mourn the death of Jesus, it is as if God and the Church wish to console us by the gift of the Eucharist. On this Good Friday, we are grateful for Jesus' death on the Cross and for receiving Him in Communion.

Points to Ponder

Jesus speaks from the Cross. He says, "Father, forgive them" (Luke 23:34). Whom do you need to forgive?

Jesus tells John to behold his mother (John 19:27). How have you taken Mary into your home?

Jesus entrusted His life into the Father's hands. How do you surrender to God's will?

Jesus, at every Mass I behold and adore Your Body and Blood in the Eucharist. Today, I behold Your body and blood, crucified and poured out for me. Thank You for the gift of salvation. Thank You for allowing me to unite myself to You in Holy Communion.

Celebrating the Eucharist after the Crucifixion

At the end of the movie *Risen*, a theatrical account of the Lord's Resurrection, when the empty tomb was discovered, one of the apostles knew exactly what they were supposed to do: they gathered and broke bread together, just as Jesus had commanded them on the night of the Last Supper. Who knows if this is what really happened, but for me, this movie scene emphasized the reality that Jesus is present in the Eucharist.

I can only imagine what was going through the minds of the apostles after the Crucifixion. Peter had denied Jesus. All but John the Beloved had abandoned Jesus in His dying hour. I am sure the apostles were overcome with grief, remorse, and fear. To hear that the tomb was empty and that Mary Magdalene had spoken with the Lord must have brought them joy and relief. And not yet having encountered the risen Christ, celebrating the Eucharist together could have made them feel like a community again. When Jesus appeared to them after the Resurrection, they had another opportunity to tell Him how much they loved Him. They could hear His voice and those ever-familiar words, "Do not be afraid."

Meditations after Holy Communion

When similar worries or fears would overcome the apostles after the Resurrection, it would be in the breaking of the bread that they would find their strength, peace, and hope as they continued to follow Jesus' teachings and make them known throughout the world.

Points to Ponder

Imagine what it was like for the apostles in those hours after Jesus died. What did they do? How did they cope? How would you have coped?

What was the apostles' reaction when they first heard about the empty tomb? Was it unbelief? Joy? When they saw Jesus for the first time after the Resurrection, what were their emotions?

What would you think or feel if you saw Jesus right now? Jesus said to the apostles, "Peace be with you." Hear Jesus say those words to your heart and soul right now.

Jesus, thank You for the gift of the Eucharist. I know that I am never alone when I receive You. You are as actually present to me as You were when you appeared to the apostles after the Resurrection. Give me Your grace and peace.

Let Jesus Speak to You

There are many accounts of our Lord's Resurrection. They are all beautiful and tell us one thing: that Jesus is risen! The tomb was empty. He was not there. He defeated death and the grave. Mary Magdalene plays a central role in the Resurrection story. She is the one who discovers the empty tomb and announces it to Jesus' apostles. In one of the Resurrection accounts, Mary Magdalene converses with someone in the garden. She assumes that the man is a gardener and that he must have taken the body of Jesus or knows where it is. But Mary Magdalene is speaking to Jesus. And she realizes it when Jesus says her name: "Mary." She responds by calling Him "Rabboni," which means "teacher." In hearing her name, she knows it is Jesus.

Every Sunday, we come to Mass, and we hear the same words, "This is my Body.... This is my Blood." And in the elevation of the Host, we see Jesus present among us. Do we hear those words? Do we allow that reality to sink in? Do we recognize it is Jesus? When the priest celebrates Mass, and especially at the Consecration, he acts in the person of Christ: it is Jesus who speaks those words of consecration at Mass as well as the words of absolution in the confessional. At Mass, listen for the voice of Jesus. You will hear His words in the Gospel proclaimed and at the Consecration. But Jesus wants to speak to you personally. Just as He spoke to Mary Magdalene in the garden, Jesus wants to speak to you in the silence of your heart. Listen for His voice.

Points to Ponder

Use your imagination. Place yourself in the garden. You begin to speak to Jesus, and then He says your name. What do you think? How do you respond? Spend a few moments repeating the name of Jesus. Take a breath in and say "Jesus"; then let the breath out and say "Jesus."

How have you heard God speak to you? Recall such a graceful moment and experience the joy of hearing again what Jesus said to you in the past.

How do you listen for Jesus' voice? How do you think He will speak to you this week?

Jesus, when You rose from the dead, You appeared to Mary Magdalene and comforted her by saying her name. Thank You for the peace You give me when I receive You in Holy Communion. In the stillness now, I listen for You to speak, and I am confident that You hear me.

Second Sunday of Easter: Divine Mercy Sunday

Jesus, I Trust in You!

A Polish nun named St. Faustina received visions of Jesus, and He relayed to her many messages. She recorded her account in her diary, *Divine Mercy in My Soul*. These private revelations received popular attention because of a Polish cardinal who was elected pope—taking the name of John Paul II. In the diary, Jesus details much about His merciful love, teaches a special chaplet, and requests that an image of Divine Mercy be painted and that a special feast of mercy be celebrated on the second Sunday of Easter. Anyone who is familiar with the Divine Mercy image knows that at the bottom of the depiction of Jesus with red and white rays coming forth from His heart are the words "Jesus, I trust in You." These are words that we all need to see, hear, pray, and repeat from time to time.

On Divine Mercy Sunday, the Gospel of "Doubting Thomas" is read. When we experience doubt, we need greater trust in Jesus. All the apostles were gathered in the Upper Room out of fear. When fear befalls us, we need greater trust in Jesus. We need trust when it comes to the sacraments of the Church: Jesus, I trust that You are present in the Holy Eucharist. Jesus, I trust that You forgive me when I confess my sins in the sacrament of Penance. On this Divine Mercy Sunday, let's pray that each day we may have a deeper trust in and dependence on Jesus.

Points to Ponder

What are some doubts you face? Do these doubts pertain to God or to the teachings of the Church?

What are some fears you have? Are there people in your life you don't trust? How can you work on trusting those people?

Jesus, because I have received You in the Holy Eucharist, I trust in You. I know that You are with me and will never abandon me. When I am overcome with fear and doubt, deepen my trust in You.

Third Sunday of Easter

Stay with Us, Lord

Luke's Gospel recounts the story of two disciples on the road to Emmaus. They are going home from Jerusalem. They've heard the news about Jesus, that He was crucified, but they've also heard that some women went to the tomb and found it empty, and this was confirmed by Jesus' apostles. We know this because the disciples recount these happenings to a stranger who draws near to them on their journey. The stranger happens to be Jesus, whom they do not recognize. Jesus then interprets for the two men all the passages of the Old Testament that referred to Him and how they were fulfilled. Once they reach Emmaus, the two disciples ask Jesus to stay with them as evening draws near. Jesus sits down at table and breaks bread, blesses it, and gives it to them. Then they recognize Him, but He disappears from their sight.

Jesus stays with us. Like those two disciples, we ask Jesus to stay with us on our journey of life. We want Jesus to walk with us. The fact is, He does; He never leaves us. He's present in the church, reserved in the Blessed Sacrament in the tabernacle. Anytime we have a problem or a worry, we can stop by our parish church and pray to Him (assuming the church doors are open).

Meditations after Holy Communion

We also know that Jesus stays with us in the Holy Communion we receive. Let's strive to be like those disciples on the road to Emmaus and never let Jesus leave our side.

Points to Ponder

If you could walk with Jesus, what would you tell Him? What do you think Jesus would say to you? Allow that to play out in your imagination. Are there any questions you want to ask Him? What are they? How have you noticed Jesus staying with you throughout your day, your week, your life? In the coming week, pay attention to Christ's nearness to you.

Padre Pio (St. Pio of Pietrelcina) wrote a beautiful prayer called Stay with Me (the text follows today's prayer). For further prayer and meditation, you may wish to pray that prayer slowly and see how each line of it speaks to you. Talk to Jesus about each line. Pay attention to what He says or does in your soul.

Jesus, now that I have received You in Holy Communion, I ask You to stay with me, not only in this moment but throughout the day and the week. As with those two disciples whose hearts burned with love for You, set my heart aflame with love and devotion to You in the Holy Eucharist.

Stay with Me
by St. Pio of Pietrelcina

Stay with me, Lord, for it is necessary to have You present so that I do not forget You. You know how easily I abandon You.

Stay with me, Lord, because I am weak and I need Your strength, that I may not fall so often.

Stay with me, Lord, for You are my life, and without You I am without fervor.

Stay with me, Lord, for You are my light, and without You I am in darkness.

Stay with me, Lord, to show me Your will.

Stay with me, Lord, so that I hear Your voice and follow You.

Stay with me, Lord, for I desire to love You very much and always be in Your company.

Stay with me, Lord, if You wish me to be faithful to You.

Stay with me, Lord; as poor as my soul is, I want it to be a place of consolation for You, a nest of love.

Stay with me, Jesus, for it is getting late and the day is coming to a close and life passes; death, judgment, and eternity approach. It is necessary to renew my strength so that I will not stop along the way, and for that, I need You.

It is getting late, and death approaches; I fear the darkness, the temptations, the dryness, the cross, the sorrows. Oh, how I need You, my Jesus, in this night of exile!

Stay with me tonight, Jesus; in life with all its dangers, I need You. Let me recognize You as Your

*disciples did at the breaking of the bread so that the
Eucharistic Communion may be the Light which
disperses the darkness, the force which sustains me, the
unique joy of my heart.*

*Stay with me, Lord, because at the hour of my
death, I want to remain united to You, if not by
Communion, at least by grace and love.*

*Stay with me, Lord, for it is You alone I look for,
Your Love, Your Grace, Your Will, Your Heart, Your
Spirit, because I love You and ask no other reward but
to love You more and more. With a firm love, I will love
You with all my heart while on earth and continue to
love You perfectly during all eternity. Amen.*

Jesus Feeds His Sheep

The Fourth Sunday of Easter receives the special designation of Good Shepherd Sunday. In the Gospels, Jesus calls Himself the Good Shepherd, for He is the shepherd of our souls. Recall how many times Jesus fed people during His public ministry and even after the Resurrection. There are the stories of the multiplication of the loaves, when Jesus realized the hunger of the people and wanted to provide for them. Making use of what was available to Him, He fed thousands with five loaves and two fish. He fed His apostles on the night of the Last Supper when He broke the bread, said the blessing, and gave them Communion. He fed the disciples on the road to Emmaus when He broke bread with them. And He fed the apostles on the shore of the Sea of Galilee after the Resurrection. Jesus looked out for people's needs, especially their physical needs, whether that meant healing or making sure they were fed.

Every Sunday when we come to Mass, Jesus feeds us. The Liturgy of the Word (the readings from Scripture, the homily, the Creed, and the petitions) is often called "the table of the word" which evokes the image of being fed with God's holy Word. The words of Scripture feed our minds and our souls. And then we are fed by Jesus at the table of the Eucharist with His Body and Blood. Just as a shepherd feeds his sheep daily and they listen to his voice, at Mass today, we have listened to Jesus speak to us and allowed Him to feed us. Be sure to savor it.

Points to Ponder

What was one thing from the Scripture readings or the homily today that fed your soul? Let that phrase or thought stay with you throughout the week and become something you try to live out or put into practice.

Do you listen to the voice of the Good Shepherd? Are there unhealthy media or foods you consume on a daily basis? Do you allow Jesus to feed your hunger for the good you desire?

Thank You, Jesus, for being the Good Shepherd who feeds His sheep and for nourishing my mind, body, and soul with Your sacred food.

Fifth Sunday of Easter

Remembering My First Holy Communion

A rite of passage in the Faith is making our First Holy Communion. Pope St. Pius X lowered the age for receiving First Communion to the age of reason, which has been determined to be about seven. Maybe you have had the opportunity to celebrate a First Communion with a family member or your parish community. It is always a special occasion for all involved.

Most children receive their First Communion with their friends and classmates. For me, that wasn't the case. I broke out in chicken pox on that momentous occasion and had to make my First Communion by myself. It was Mother's Day weekend that year and a day removed from my birthday. My hometown pastor was on vacation that weekend, so a visiting priest gave me Jesus for the first time. I have pictures from that day and also from another Mass, where I dressed up again in the same clothes to receive Jesus from our pastor. Pictures document that occasion too.

Meditations after Holy Communion

Points to Ponder

What do you remember about your First Holy
Communion? At what church did it take
place? Who was the priest? Did you have a
profound experience with Jesus that day?

What was your second Holy Communion like? In
your imagination, try to relive that experience of
yours. And if you can't call it to mind, think of a
First Communion you have been to recently.

*Thank You, Jesus, for allowing me to receive You in
Holy Communion. Ever since my First Communion,
I have been able to be united to You in a special way.
Help me to appreciate every Communion with the faith
of a child, who so readily believes that You are truly
present.*

Sixth Sunday of Easter

Help Me to Love

In the breviary, the prayers that priests, deacons, and religious promise to pray daily, there is an antiphon for the feast of an apostle that always makes me pause and think: "You are my friends if you do what I command you." Every time I encounter that sentence, I ask myself, "Am I a friend of Jesus? Do I do what He has commanded me?" We know the Ten Commandments as given to Moses, which Jesus summarizes as loving God and neighbor. In Matthew 25, Jesus commands us to love those who are hungry, naked, sick, imprisoned, and the list goes on. He also commands us to love our enemies and do good to those who hate us. How are you doing with living the commandments and teachings of Jesus?

If you are like me, you probably have someone in your life you find it hard to love. It might be a family member, a co-worker, or an acquaintance. That person may have hurt you in some way, might have done something to you or said something to you or about you, and it is difficult to want what is good for him or her. Despite all that, you are called to love that person. What does that mean? It means that you should want that person to get to Heaven and want nothing less for him or her.

Meditations after Holy Communion

Jesus commands us to love. As we receive the Holy Eucharist, which is called the sacrament of charity, let us pray that it will set our hearts on fire with love for all people, friend and foe.

Points to Ponder

Whom do you find it difficult to love? What did they do to you that requires God's healing? Pray for that healing grace. Do you need to repent of any unloving actions toward that individual? Do you love your enemy? Have you carried out charitable actions toward your neighbor?

Jesus, I know that You love me because You died for me. And now You give Yourself to me in the Eucharist I receive. Remove all hatred and bitterness from my heart and help me to love those whom I find it difficult to love. Help me to will their good and want eternal life for them.

Seventh Sunday of Easter and the Ascension of the Lord

Jesus Wants Us to Go!

Do you know what the word "Mass" means? It means "sent." It comes from the Latin word *missa*, used in the final words of the Mass (in Latin): *Ite, missa est* (Go, you are sent). In the Ordinary Form of the Mass, there are four options the priest or deacon can use to dismiss the people: (1) "Go forth, the Mass is ended"; (2) "Go in peace"; (3) "Go and announce the gospel of the Lord"; (4) "Go in peace, glorifying the Lord by your life." In each one of these dismissals, the word "go" is used. Maybe at the end of Mass, you are grateful to hear those words because you are ready to go on to the next event of the day. But those words truly make you a missionary. Listen for them at Mass. Don't ignore them. Take them as your marching orders.

Each week, we come to Mass and are nourished with the Word of God and receive the Holy Eucharist. In one sense, we can see this as a way for us to be refreshed spiritually and strengthened by God's grace for the coming week. After all that God does for us during the Mass, both visibly and invisibly, we are exhorted at the end of Mass to go. This is, in part, because we have become configured more closely to Christ. We received Him into our very bodies and carry Him within us. When we are told to go in peace and glorify the Lord by our lives, it's a reminder to us that God has changed us in that hour at Mass and we are to be different. If we come to Mass each week and remain the same person, then what is it worth? Each week, the Eucharist and the Mass must remind us of who God calls us to become and must encourage us to live the grace of the Holy Mass.

After you leave church and throughout the week, you will go to many places. Wherever you go—whether home, or to a restaurant, or to school or work—remember that you are to announce the gospel and glorify the Lord by your life.

Points to Ponder

What did you think about today when Mass ended and you heard the words "Go in peace"? Did you hear the words, or were you on autopilot?

Where will you go today? How will you proclaim the gospel? In what ways do you glorify God by your life right now? In what ways do you need to change to glorify the Lord better?

How has your friendship with Jesus changed you?

Jesus, I have received You and am so grateful. Knowing that You are with me gives me the strength to serve You and my neighbor this week. By the grace of this Holy Eucharist, may my words and actions be always pleasing to You, proclaim Your gospel, and glorify You.

Pentecost

The Power of the Holy Spirit

All seven sacraments of the Catholic Church call down the power of the Holy Spirit. This calling down in Greek is called the epiclesis. At every Mass, this occurs when the priest stretches his hands out over the bread and wine. Eucharistic Prayer III says, "Therefore, O Lord, we humbly implore you: by the same Spirit graciously make holy these gifts we have brought to you for consecration." The Holy Spirit possesses the power to sanctify. During Mass, as we attend, pray, and receive the Eucharist, we can ask the Holy Spirit to make us, God's people, holy.

The Holy Spirit plays a major role in the lives of all Christians. Through Baptism and Confirmation, we all have received the Holy Spirit, who brings us seven gifts: wisdom, understanding, counsel, fortitude, knowledge, piety, and fear of the Lord.[1] As Catholics, we are called to live the fruits of the Holy Spirit: charity, joy, peace, patience, kindness, goodness, generosity, gentleness, faithfulness, modesty, self-control, chastity.[2] Each day, ask

---

[1] *Catechism of the Catholic Church*, no. 1831.
[2] *Catechism of the Catholic Church*, no. 1832; see Gal. 5:22–23.

the Holy Spirit to guide you wherever you go and in whatever you do or say. Allow the Holy Spirit to inspire you. Sometimes we call these "Holy Spirit moments," when something comes to our minds, such as a person, and we reach out to that person only to find out that he or she needed someone to talk to. The Holy Spirit also reminds us of all the good that God has done throughout the day and throughout our lives. Allow the Mass to be the example for your daily life—by reminding you to call upon and live in the Holy Spirit.

Points to Ponder

Think over the last week. How was the Holy
Spirit in your life—in the events that happened
and in the conversations you had?

Think about the coming week. When do
you anticipate needing the Holy Spirit the
most? Which gift of the Holy Spirit (wisdom,
understanding, counsel, fortitude, knowledge, piety,
and fear of the Lord) do you need the most?

Thank You, Jesus, for sending the Holy Spirit upon the earth on that first Pentecost and at each celebration of the Mass. As the Holy Spirit descends upon the bread and wine before the Consecration, I ask at every Mass to receive the Holy Spirit in a powerful way. Send the Holy Spirit to sanctify, renew, guide, and inspire me at every moment of every day.

Ordinary Time

The Holy Trinity

The Father, the Son, and the Holy Spirit

Every Mass begins with the Sign of the Cross, invoking the triune God, who is Father, Son, and Holy Spirit. Have you ever noticed the construction of the prayers at Mass? We direct them to God the Father, through Jesus, His Son, and in unity with the Holy Spirit. It happens in the opening prayer, called the Collect, in the Preface, in the Eucharistic Prayer, and in many of the prayers of the Mass. When the apostles asked Jesus how they should pray, He taught them the Our Father, giving them and us an example of what to say as we praise God as Father and make our requests.

How do you pray? Which person of the Blessed Trinity do you usually address? Maybe you call upon God as Father; maybe you also talk with Jesus. This book is meant to teach you to converse with Jesus after Holy Communion. When was the last time you asked the Holy Spirit, with whom you were sealed on the day of your Confirmation, to assist you? As you pray this week, consider praying as the priest does at Mass: address your prayer to God the Father, and offer it through Jesus and in union with the Holy Spirit. Pay attention to the different ways you pray this week, and notice how you invoke the Trinity.

Meditations after Holy Communion

Points to Ponder

Have you ever paused to reflect on what the
Sign of the Cross means? How attentively
do you listen to the prayers at Mass, such as
the Opening Prayer after the Gloria?

What does your daily prayer life look like?
Do you use scripted prayers, or do you talk to
God in your own words? Which person of the
Blessed Trinity do you normally address?

Have you recently asked God to help to
make use of the seven gifts of the Holy Spirit
or to live the fruits of the Holy Spirit?

*Father, thank You for sending Your Son, Jesus, to save
us from our sins and to institute the Holy Eucharist.
You sent forth the Holy Spirit today to sanctify the
bread and wine, and I give You thanks for the gift of the
Holy Eucharist.*

The Most Holy Body and Blood of Jesus Christ

The Sacrament of Unity

⬧

The Eucharist has been called the sacrament of unity. After all, on the night before Jesus died, He prayed that all might be one. Today, there are many divisions in the Body of Christ. And not all Christian believers hold the same belief about the Holy Eucharist—namely, that it is the Body, Blood, Soul, and Divinity of Jesus. We pray that one day we all may be one and experience true unity in the Body of Christ.

Another kind of unity is our personal union with Jesus in the sacrament because He comes to us and we receive Him. The Mass also unites us to the liturgy in Heaven and to those who have gone before us in faith. In his book *The Lamb's Supper*, Dr. Scott Hahn beautifully describes the liturgy of Heaven as detailed in the book of Revelation. We hear such language in the Mass in the Preface, as the priest says that we join the angels and saints in their unending hymn of praise, which leads us into the Holy, Holy, Holy. All the angels and the saints participate in praising God when we celebrate the Mass. This means that we are united with our loved ones who preceded us in death (assuming they enjoy the Beatific Vision of Heaven).

Meditations after Holy Communion

The Mass we celebrate as Catholics unites us with believers throughout the world who are participating in the same prayer in their own languages. We are also united with our Holy Father and our bishop.

Next time you are at Mass, during the Lamb of God, watch for the priest to break a small piece off the Host and drop it into the chalice. This small gesture recalls a practice from long ago acknowledging that the Mass was celebrated in union with the local bishop. Finally, the Eucharist binds us to service to the poor. St. John Chrysostom said, "If you can't see Jesus in the beggar at the church door, how do you expect to see Him in the chalice?" My time at Mundelein Seminary introduced me to a figure in the Liturgical Movement named Fr. Reginald Hildebrand. His major contribution was to link the Eucharist with social justice and action. The Eucharist, as the sacrament of unity, compels us to serve Christ, whom we meet in the poor.

Points to Ponder

The Eucharist is the sacrament of unity. Where do you experience division in your life?

The Mass unites us to those in Heaven. Which saint or deceased person do you wish to pray in union with during the Mass? What do you picture Heaven to be like?

Do you seek to be in union with the pope or your bishop, or do you find yourself at odds with the institutional Church?

The Sacrament of Unity

How have you been united to Christ
in your service to the poor?

*Thank You, Jesus, for letting me be united to You
through the reception of Holy Communion. Help me
always to foster unity and not division. Lead me where
You want me to go, and show me how You wish me to
serve my brother or sister in need.*

Second Sunday in Ordinary Time

Affirmation of Belief

In the introduction, I shared how this book came about: first, through my devotional prayer at the Elevation, "Truly it is You," which served as a reminder of the reality of what takes place at Mass, and second, through my discovery of Fr. Daniel Lord's book *Christ in Me*. Both of these motivations emphasize the importance of our acceptance of Christ's presence in the Holy Eucharist.

Statistics show that the majority of Catholics do not understand the Eucharist. They do not believe that the Eucharist is truly the Body, Blood, Soul, and Divinity of Jesus. Instead, they might believe it is a symbol or a representation, but they do not accept the literal words of Jesus at the Last Supper. Maybe you have doubts or reservations about the Eucharist. If you do, know that that is okay for now, but it is important to work through them. We must not remain in doubt and disbelief. Take steps toward understanding Jesus' presence in the Eucharist. Praying with this book after Mass is one of the steps you already are taking.

Many saints wrote about the Eucharist. Contemporary authors, such as Vinny Flynn (*Seven Secrets of the Eucharist*), break open the mystery of the Eucharist for readers. Learn about the

Eucharist and why we Catholics believe what we believe. Learn the stories of the Eucharistic miracles that are still on display throughout the world as a sign of Christ's Real Presence. And most importantly, whatever your doubt might be, ask God to give you a stronger belief in the Holy Eucharist.

Points to Ponder

Do you believe that Jesus is truly and really present in the Holy Eucharist? If not, what is your main point of contention? How can you move from doubt to faith?

Lord Jesus, I believe You are present in the Eucharist, but in moments of doubt, help my unbelief. Every time I receive You in Holy Communion, may it always strengthen my belief in Your presence.

Third Sunday in Ordinary Time

Are You Prepared?

There is a certain amount of preparation that goes into most tasks we undertake. If I am writing a book or a paper, I have to do some reading and research before I outline and write the text. If I am making a meal, I need to prepare by taking necessary items out of the freezer or going to the store to buy the ingredients. How do we prepare for Sunday Mass? We put on our Sunday best. We get into the right mindset, preparing ourselves for where we are going and what we will experience. Reading the Scripture readings in advance will help us to hear the Word of God proclaimed and to understand better the homily the priest or deacon will preach. On the way to Mass, we might get into a holier mindset by listening to Christian music, praying with our family, or talking about godly things. We might also celebrate the sacrament of Reconciliation prior to Sunday.

As you reflect now after attending Mass today, how well were you prepared? How will you prepare for your holy encounter next weekend?

Meditations after Holy Communion

Points to Ponder

What did you do to prepare for Sunday
Mass this weekend? Was there any spiritual
preparation? If not, why didn't you prepare?
Were you too busy? Rushed in the morning?

What would your ideal preparation look like?
Create a checklist so you will know what you would
like to accomplish before next Sunday's Mass.

*Lord Jesus, in the busyness of life, sometimes I take
Mass and the gift of the Eucharist for granted. Help me
to slow down so that I can better appreciate what it is I
celebrate and be prepared for my Eucharistic encounter.*

Fourth Sunday in Ordinary Time

Remembering God's Love

Have you ever paused to consider how much God loves you? You might have had specific moments or experiences in which you were overwhelmed by God's love. It could have been after the celebration of Mass or after Confession or at a time when God spared you some misfortune. It also could have been in the small things in life. When I sit outside during the summer and watch the sunset or look at the beauty of nature, I become awed that God loves me so much that I am able to take in His created wonders.

In the spiritual life, it is important for us never to forget these occasions of grace. Remembering these moments should move us to give thanks to God for the blessings He allowed us to receive. Each time we are privileged to receive the Holy Eucharist, that, too, is a moment of overwhelming love, when Jesus, who loves us so much, comes to us sacramentally. Let every Sunday be a reminder of God's love through the Sacrament of Charity, which is the Eucharist.

Meditations after Holy Communion

Points to Ponder

When was the last time you told the Lord how much you love Him? Do you ever think about God's love for you? Recall one experience where you were overwhelmed by how much God loves you. Allow that to begin a conversation with God in which you express your love and gratitude and commit yourself to loving Him more.

Father, thank You for loving us so much that You gave Your Son, Jesus, to the world to die on the Cross. Thank You for loving me so much that now I am able to receive Jesus in Holy Communion. Fill me with Your divine love so that I will never forget how much You love me and that I will see how Your love surrounds me every day.

Fifth Sunday in Ordinary Time

A Song of Praise

I sometimes pray my Holy Hour after Mass. This means I stay in the church and pray before the tabernacle in various ways and in personal conversation with God. On one occasion, as I prayed my Holy Hour, my heart was so filled with gratitude that I burst into song using a classic hymn many people know, "How Great Thou Art." Luckily, I was the only person in the church, but that was the movement of my soul that day. I wanted to praise God in song and proclaim His greatness. The words of the hymn capture my experience: "Then sings my soul, my savior God, to Thee."

I'm willing to bet that sometimes you break out in song throughout the day as you go about your work. It might be a song you heard on the radio, and for whatever reason, you want to sing that song in that moment. And I'm sure we have all found ourselves, on occasion, humming the last song from Mass, especially if it was catchy.

Song expresses our emotions. In the encounter of Mary and Elizabeth in the Visitation and Mary's proclaiming the greatness of God (in her Magnificat), we like to imagine that Mary broke out in song. Men and women religious in monasteries throughout the world chant Mary's song of praise each evening. What Mary teaches us in the Visitation is that her soul was moved to break out in prayer because John the Baptist recognized the presence of Christ and Elizabeth called her blessed among women. As we encounter Christ's sacramental presence, let us also break out in praise.

Points to Ponder

What is it like for you to receive Holy Communion? Do you notice a stirring of joy afterward? Are you filled with thanksgiving?

Do you sing the Communion song louder after receiving Communion? Allow God to inspire a song of praise in your heart and soul after each week's encounter.

My soul magnifies the Lord,
and my spirit rejoices in God my Savior,
for he has regarded the low estate of his
*   handmaiden.*
For behold, henceforth all generations will call
*   me blessed;*
for he who is mighty has done great things for me,
and holy is his name.
And his mercy is on those who fear him
from generation to generation.
He has shown strength with his arm,
he has scattered the proud in the imagination
*   of their hearts,*

A Song of Praise

he has put down the mighty from their thrones,
and exalted those of low degree;
he has filled the hungry with good things,
and the rich he has sent empty away.
He has helped his servant Israel,
in remembrance of his mercy,
as he spoke to our fathers,
to Abraham and to his posterity for ever.
(Luke 1:46–55)

Sixth Sunday in Ordinary Time

Calm the Storm of My Life

During the COVID-19 pandemic, Pope Francis stood in an empty St. Peter's Basilica in Vatican City. The Gospel chanted by the minister was the account of the apostles on a stormy sea while Jesus was asleep. During that homily, Pope Francis called upon Jesus and asked Him to wake up, as so many throughout the world were suffering. At one point, he called upon Our Lady as the Star of the Stormy Sea.

At times, we can probably relate to the apostles, who called out to Jesus to wake up. They were afraid because of the storm they faced. Our lives are filled with storms and fears as well: the unexpected illness or death of a loved one, the loss of a job, or some other unforeseen circumstance. We all have faced the stormy waters of life. Maybe you are just coming out of a storm or are in the midst of a storm, or unbeknownst to you, you are entering one right now. Or if you are fortunate, I hope, you are coasting along on calm waters.

If you are in a storm, or the next time you find yourself at rock bottom, know that Jesus is with you. He has your back. With a few words, He calmed the storm at sea. He will calm the storm of your life. Have recourse to Jesus' power and mercy. Call out to Him. Ask Him to calm the stormy waters you face.

Points to Ponder

Do you feel as if you are sinking? Did you
have a bad week? Spend time talking to Jesus
about whatever is going on in your life.

Are you experiencing the calmness of life? Think of a
time when you were sinking and how God rescued you.

*Jesus, You calmed the fears of the apostles. Bring me
peace of mind in whatever I face. When I am at a low
in my life, let me not forget to turn to You and draw
strength from the Holy Eucharist.*

Seventh Sunday in Ordinary Time

Give Me Strength for the Week

A couple told me once that their child asked one Sunday morning, "Do we really have to go to Mass today?" I presume it was a busy weekend. Maybe they had sporting events scheduled all weekend. But the family made time for Sunday Mass. The answer the parents gave the child was, "Going to church is our fill-up for the week."

Sunday Mass gives us the encouragement and grace we need to get ourselves through the week. When public Masses were suspended during the COVID-19 pandemic, Catholics throughout the world were unable to receive their weekly sustenance and nourishment, and many reflected that they felt the loss.

We come to Mass, each Mass, with so many experiences. Each week is different. We could mourn one week and be celebrating a promotion the next. And God has a message for us each week in the Word of God we hear proclaimed. And sometimes it is just the message we need to hear.

When you are weighed down by the stresses of daily life, ask Jesus at Mass to help you through the week. Bring Him your worries and concerns, and ask Him to lighten your load.

Meditations after Holy Communion

Points to Ponder

What do the next seven days look like for you? Is there
something you are dreading? What are you looking
forward to? Where will you need God's help the most
this week? As you answer these questions, ask God to
help you and be with you. As you go through the week,
remember, God's grace is helping you along the way.

*Thank You, Jesus, for allowing me to receive You in
Holy Communion. From You I draw the strength I
need each day. Whatever I face this week, let me face it
with grace, knowing that You are with me.*

Eighth Sunday in Ordinary Time

Anima Christi

As I shared in the introduction, one of the first prayers I began praying after Holy Communion, and the one I still pray, is the Anima Christi. For the longest time, it was believed that St. Ignatius of Loyola (1491–1556) wrote the prayer because he includes it in *The Spiritual Exercises*. The author is unknown, but the prayer is speculated to have been written before St. Ignatius's time and is sometimes attributed to Pope John XXII (1244–1334). You may even hear the prayer sung as the hymn "Soul of My Savior." Let's take a look at the prayer line by line:

> Soul of Christ, sanctify me.
> Body of Christ, save me.
> Blood of Christ, inebriate me.
> Water from the side of Christ, wash me.
> Passion of Christ, strengthen me.
> O good Jesus, hear me.
> Within Thy wounds hide me.
> Suffer me not to be separated from Thee.
> From the malignant enemy defend me.

In the hour of my death call me.
And bid me come unto Thee.
That with Thy saints I may praise Thee
Forever and ever.
Amen.

Encapsulated in the prayer are many requests. We ask Jesus to sanctify us, meaning that we want Him to make us holy. The Eucharist sanctifies us and invites us to a deeper holiness. *Jesus, save me by the blood Your body poured out*. It might seem odd to ask to be inebriated, but think of Cana and how Jesus turns water into wine. We ask Him to inebriate us with joy. In asking to be washed, we acknowledge the cleansing nature of the Eucharist to forgive our venial sins. Jesus strengthens us for our daily tasks and in times of trial. From His Passion, we take inspiration. By Holy Communion we are united with Christ, and so we ask not to be separated from Him by sin. We wish to stay close to Jesus. In our struggle against evil, the Eucharist becomes the power we draw upon to be defended from the enemy. And then we call to mind our death, knowing that Jesus will call us and invite us to the banquet feast of Heaven with all His saints, for this is the promise for those who eat His Body and drink His Blood. With so many who have prayed this prayer throughout the years, we pray it today, asking Jesus to manifest His power in our lives.

Points to Ponder

Focus on each petition of the Anima Christi
and talk to Jesus about it. How can you become
holier? Where do you need strength? How has
Jesus heard you in the past, and what do you want

Him to hear specifically today? Which saint do you want to take your place next to in Heaven?

Jesus, thank You for allowing me to receive Holy Communion and for all that You accomplish in me through Your presence. Sanctify me, strengthen me, hear me, and defend me this day as I strive to run the race of life before me.

Ninth Sunday in Ordinary Time

What Holy Communion Does for Us

In Catholic prayer books and hand missals, a common prayer for after Communion penned by St. Thomas Aquinas can be found (see today's prayer). St. Thomas had a deep devotion to the Holy Eucharist and wrote the prayers for the Mass of Corpus Christi. He is one of the intellectual giants of the Catholic Faith because of his tomes of theological writings. Yet one time, when he was praying before the Blessed Sacrament, he said to the Lord (and I paraphrase), "Everything I have written is like straw compared with what I have seen and what has been revealed to me." He understood the mysteries of God but also knew the mysteries behind all the dogma and doctrine.

The prayer St. Thomas penned for after Communion conveys teachings about the Eucharist and what the Eucharist accomplishes in those who receive it. It is a saving plea for forgiveness, an armor of faith, and a shield of goodwill. After Holy Communion, we can ask Jesus for help to conquer the vices in our lives and for an increase in virtue. The Eucharist we receive prepares us for our eternal destiny in Heaven, and the pure joy we experience after receiving Holy Communion is a foretaste of Heaven.

Meditations after Holy Communion

Heaven is a place of eternal joy and happiness, because we will be in the presence of Jesus forever.

Points to Ponder

What vices or bad habits do you need to empty yourself of? Do you need an increase of charity, patience, humility, obedience, or any other virtue? Which one do you want to work on this week?

What do you think of when you picture Heaven? Do you see it as an eternal banquet? A place of happiness?

Prayer of St. Thomas Aquinas after Holy Communion

I thank You, O Holy Lord, Almighty Father, Eternal God, who have deigned, not through any merits of mine, but out of the condescension of Your goodness, to satisfy me, a sinner, Your unworthy servant, with the precious Body and Blood of Your Son, our Lord Jesus Christ.

I pray that this Holy Communion be not a condemnation to punishment for me, but a saving plea to forgiveness. May it be to me the armor of faith and the shield of goodwill. May it be the emptying out of my vices and the extinction of all lustful desires; an increase of charity and patience, of humility and obedience, and all virtues; a strong defense against the snares of all my enemies, visible and invisible; the perfect quieting of all my evil impulses of flesh and spirit, binding me firmly to

You, the one true God; and a happy ending of my life. I pray, too, that You will deign to bring me, a sinner, to that ineffable banquet where You, with Your Son and the Holy Spirit, are to Your saints true light, fulfillment of desires, eternal joy, unalloyed gladness, and perfect bliss. Through the same Christ our Lord. Amen.

Tenth Sunday in Ordinary Time

Heal Me, Lord!

Just before Communion, we pray, "Lord I am not worthy that you should enter under my roof, but only say the word and my soul shall be healed." We know that these are the words uttered by the Roman centurion as he asked Jesus to heal his servant (see Matt. 8:8). Those humble words have been repeated for centuries now and by each one of us.

"But only say the word, and my soul shall be healed." Jesus wants to heal us. It's the very reason He died on the Cross: to heal the world of the effects of sin and to right what was wrong. Every Sunday, we acknowledge our need for healing from Jesus. Those battling illness or terminal disease seek physical healing. For others, it is the healing from emotional wounds with which they have been afflicted. We might ask Jesus to heal a broken friendship or a relationship with someone. Jesus is the Divine Physician, and through the Eucharist, He offers us medicine for our souls.

There was an elderly gentleman from my home parish (he has since passed on to eternal life), who shared with me a healing he experienced through the Eucharist. He had been experiencing some bleeding in his mouth. As he received Holy Communion one day, he moved the Host to the affected area. The bleeding that day stopped immediately. Like you and me, he had just prayed those words prior to receiving Holy Communion: "only say the word, and my soul shall be healed." That day he experienced a bodily healing through the Eucharist. Today, ask Jesus to heal you in body and soul.

Points to Ponder

Do you need healing? What type of healing?
Physical? Spiritual? Emotional? Psychological?
Don't be afraid to ask Jesus to heal you. Where or
why do you hurt right now? What is broken? Do
you know your woundedness? Spend time thinking
about the type of healing you need, and ask Jesus
for it. You might also wish to bring to the Lord
someone you know who is in need of healing.

*Lord Jesus, only say the word, and I shall be healed. I
desire to be healed of all my infirmities and brokenness.
As the Divine Physician, please give me Your healing
grace.*

Eleventh Sunday in Ordinary Time

Give Me Joy!

Joy surrounds Jesus. Put another way, Jesus brings joy. There's no biblical scene where this is more evident than the Visitation, when Mary and Elizabeth greet each other and John the Baptist leaps for joy in the womb. The presence of Christ brings joy.

The same was true for me when I celebrated Mass for a congregation of sisters. My first priestly assignment had me celebrating Mass for the community two or three times a week. I would bring Communion to the infirm nuns who could not walk up for Holy Communion. There was one sister who had difficulty communicating because of her advanced dementia. She would hum songs every once in a while, but rarely could she converse. Each time I brought her Holy Communion and said, "The Body of Christ," a little smile came over her face. She knew who was visiting her: it was the Lord Jesus, the One to whom she was espoused as a consecrated religious. I see this when I bring Communion to the homebound: their eyes well up with tears of joy because they are able to receive the Lord Jesus in Holy Communion.

When we come to Mass on Sunday, we might be burdened with the activities of life, and maybe some circumstances cause us sadness. Let us pray for the grace each time we approach to receive Holy Communion that we will have smiles on our faces and that the Lord Jesus will fill us with joy.

Points to Ponder

What are the things in your life that cause you sadness? What is your emotional state right now? When you are sad, what brings you happiness?

Were you filled with joy when you received Holy Communion today?

How do you bring yourself out of a funky mood so that you will exude joy to others and not burden them with your sadness?

Lord Jesus, I am filled with joy because I have been able to receive You in Holy Communion. Permit my soul always to rejoice at the moment I receive You. May the Eucharist fill me with so much joy that I will be joy-filled throughout the week.

Twelfth Sunday in Ordinary Time

A Bold Request

⸺⸺⸺⸺ ❁ ⸺⸺⸺⸺

When you pray, you probably make some requests of God. You might ask Him to bless your family or help you with a task you are facing. Have you ever made a bold request of God? I have. God has come through in many ways, but there are two times I will never forget.

One Saturday morning, a little more than a year after I had been ordained, I was praying before the Blessed Sacrament. I asked Jesus, "Show me this is real." I wasn't having serious doubts or anything like that, but I needed some affirmation of the reality of the priesthood. The next evening, I was in my office finishing a paper for a conference the next day. Our Sunday evening Mass had not yet begun for the fall season, but some people showed up, including the couple who became the answer to the prayer I had made the previous day. I volunteered to celebrate Mass for the dozen people who showed up, and then the moments of grace transpired. Another Saturday morning, after experiencing a drought in confessions for about a month, I asked Jesus to send me some penitents. That night, I had a line for Confession.

In our prayer, we need to be specific and bold. Jesus taught, "Ask and you shall receive, knock and the door will be opened, seek and you will find" (see Matt. 7:7). In your prayer, ask and be bold.

Points to Ponder

What is the last petition you prayed? Have you ever been bold with God? What was the outcome? Is there something you want to ask God for right now? Be bold and do it.

Jesus, because You are with me in the Eucharist I receive, I know that this is a powerful time to talk with You. I ask You to hear my prayers that I offer this day just as You heard the prayers of people long ago. Show Yourself and bestow Your grace upon me.

In Reparation for My Sins

Popular Catholic speaker Matthew Kelly writes and talks about being the "best version of yourself." We all know that there are times when we are not the best versions of ourselves. It happens when we lose our calm or say something hurtful to a person. When you hurt a person you care about, if you are like me, you feel awful afterward and don't understand why you spoke or acted as you did. What are we to do when we hurt a friend? We try to repair the damage. We admit our wrong, apologize, and strive not to hurt that person in the future.

The same is true for our God. Each time we sin is an offense against God. And when we sin, we repair our relationship with God through sacramental Confession. When we pray the Act of Contrition, we say that we will try to avoid the near occasion of sin.

Today, Jesus comes to us in the Holy Eucharist and He wishes to heal our wounds. We tell Him in return how sorry we are and that we never want to hurt Him again.

Meditations after Holy Communion

Points to Ponder

Was there a moment this past week when you weren't the best version of yourself? Did you hurt someone by your words or actions? Are you aware of anything for which you should make reparation?

When was the last time you went to Confession? As you bring to a close your conversation with Jesus, tell Him that you never want to hurt Him again by sin, and ask Him for His help.

Jesus, I am sorry for the ways that I have hurt You and others. Please forgive me. I offer my Holy Communion as reparation for my sins, and I promise to try my best to offend You no more.

Fourteenth Sunday in Ordinary Time

In Reparation for the Sins of the World

Two of the most well-known apparitions of Jesus were received by religious sisters: St. Margaret Mary Alacoque and St. Faustina Kowalska. St. Margaret Mary popularized the devotion to Jesus' Sacred Heart, and St. Faustina received the message of Divine Mercy. Both devotions have a Eucharistic component to them.

For the Sacred Heart, St. Margaret Mary and devotees were requested to observe the Five First Fridays and receive Holy Communion in reparation for sin. The Eucharist and the Sacred Heart are also tied together in the prayer that is often prayed at the end of the Divine Praises: "May the Heart of Jesus, in the Most Blessed Sacrament, be praised, adored, and loved with grateful affection, at every moment, in all the tabernacles of the world, even to the end of time. Amen." The Eucharist is Christ's love for us, so devotion to the Sacred Heart leads us to the Eucharist. And in some Eucharistic miracles, where the Host became real flesh, studies of the Host showed it to be flesh from the heart of a dying man. This was the case with the Eucharistic miracle of Sokolka.

The prayers of the Divine Mercy Chaplet also have a Eucharistic element: "Eternal Father, I offer You the Body and Blood, Soul and Divinity of Your dearly beloved Son, our Lord, Jesus Christ, in atonement for our sins and those of the whole world." The prayer reinforces our belief in the Real Presence, acknowledging that the Eucharist is the Body, Blood, Soul, and Divinity of Jesus. It also helps us to realize our roles, in virtue of our Baptism, as priests, prophets, and kings. Through the baptismal priesthood, we are able to offer our prayers and sacrifices, and the Divine Mercy prayer does just that: "I offer You ... in atonement for our sins and those of the whole world." It is similar to the part in each Mass when the priest prays that "my sacrifice and yours" will be acceptable to God.

Both the Sacred Heart and the Divine Mercy devotions ask us to make reparation or atone for sins, and not just our sins, but those of the whole world. There are many moral evils that surround us — abortion, euthanasia, assaults against purity, racism, and the list goes on. As believers, we have the opportunity to repair and atone for the damage caused by sin. Today, as we receive the Eucharist, let us offer our Communion in reparation for the sins of the world.

Points to Ponder

Are there specific sins of the world you want to make reparation and atonement for — abortion, euthanasia, impurity, and so forth? Is there someone in particular on whose behalf you want to make reparation?

Lord Jesus, thank You for allowing me to receive the Eucharist today. I turn to You now with a heart filled with sorrow over the sins of the world. I love You so much, and I wish to atone for all the sins that offend You. Receive my humble prayer, sacrifices, and simple offerings this day, and be pleased to bestow Your mercy upon the whole world. Touch our hearts and bring everyone back to You so that they may know the love You have for them.

For the Conversion of Sinners

In 1859, the Blessed Virgin Mary appeared in Wisconsin to a Belgian immigrant named Adele Brise. Today, the National Shrine of Our Lady of Good Help commemorates the apparition, and pilgrims visit it regularly.

In the early days of October 1859, Adele saw the Blessed Mother for the first time. Unfortunately, the Blessed Mother did not say anything and quickly vanished. A few days later, on October 9, 1859, Mary appeared again to Adele. This time, Adele was on her way to church with a few of her friends. Again, Mary did not say anything. Troubled by the experience, she spoke with the parish priest, who instructed her to ask the woman, "In God's name who are you and what do you want of me?"

On her way home from Mass, Adele had the opportunity to ask the question. The woman identified herself as the Queen of Heaven, who prays for the conversion of sinners. She expressed her desire for Adele to do the same. Having just gone to Mass, Adele was commended for her reception of Holy Communion. Mary said, "You received Holy Communion this morning and that is well, but you must do more: make a general confession and offer your Communion for the conversion of sinners." At the end of the apparition, Mary instructed Adele to gather the children and teach them what they should know for salvation, how to approach the sacraments, and how to make the Sign of the Cross.

Mary's message has a sacramental emphasis. Mary asks Adele to offer her Holy Communion. This request to offer Holy Communion for a particular intention highlights the fact that the Catholic faithful unite their prayers to those of the priest, who offers the Mass in virtue of the laity's baptismal priesthood. Second, Mary tells Adele to teach the children how to approach the sacraments. Perhaps part of Adele's instruction would have been the aspect of prayerful thanksgiving following one's reception of Communion.

Points to Ponder

When you think of the conversion of sinners, does a particular person come to mind? Is it your family members who are not practicing the Faith? An atheistic co-worker? A friend who lives an immoral life? Or maybe it's a category of people, such as abortionists or those in the pornography industry. Name the person or people for whom you want to pray.

Eternal Father, I kneel before You this day with a grateful heart because You have allowed me to receive the Body and Blood of Your Son, Jesus, in Holy Communion. Thank You for sending the Queen of Heaven to earth with a message calling us to conversion and emphasizing the sacraments. When she appeared to Adele Brise in 1859, she asked Adele to offer her Holy Communion for the conversion of sinners. Just as Adele did long ago, I wish to do likewise this day.

I offer to You, Eternal Father, the Body, Blood, Soul, and Divinity of Your Son, for the conversion of sinners, including my own conversion, in reparation for sin, and for the salvation of souls. Through Our Lady's maternal solicitude, may the hearts of hardened sinners return to the sacraments of Penance and Eucharist, especially to Sunday Mass, and to daily prayer.

As I go forward from this Holy Mass, help me to fear nothing, knowing that You are with me and are always guiding me and that Our Lady constantly intercedes for me. Make me aware of Your presence this day and always. Amen.

Harvesting the Fruits

---※---

Catholic hymn writer Omer Westendorf, in the song "Sent Forth by God's Blessing," wrote this line:

> The people of God from this dwelling take leave.
> God's sacrifice ended,
> O now be extended,
> The fruits of this Mass in all hearts who believe.

I love hearing this song at the end of Mass as I recess out and the people of God return to their lives after sanctifying the day by praying at Mass and receiving the Holy Eucharist. I'm always moved by the words "the fruits of this Mass in all hearts who believe." Each time I hear them, I pause for a few moments to ponder what the fruits of the Mass I just celebrated might be. In the spiritual life, there are visible and invisible realities. And when we are at Mass on any given Sunday, we might be properly disposed or we might possibly be distraught. No matter our disposition, the invisible realities and grace are at work, and we do receive fruits from the Mass in which we participate.

Meditations after Holy Communion

What are some of the fruits of the Holy Mass? There is the fruit of having prayed—that during Mass we gave praise, glory, and honor to Almighty God and offered our sacrifice of thanksgiving. The Mass as a sacrifice perpetuates the forgiveness of sins. Whenever we encounter God's sacred Word in the Scriptures, God is at work. When St. Anthony of the Desert heard at Mass one day the Gospel passage that says, "Go, sell what you have," he did precisely that and then dedicated his life to prayer and fasting as a desert monk. Maybe today God spoke to you through the readings, and that is a fruit of this Mass. Or perhaps the homily challenged you in a new way. Other fruits could include peace of mind and heart, an increase of love, or greater confidence in a decision. The fruits of the Mass are numerous. Harvest your fruits for an abundant spiritual life.

Points to Ponder

Can you name a fruit of the Mass that you received today? Did something in the Scripture readings strike you profoundly, as a Gospel passage struck St. Anthony of the Desert? Do you believe that God is at work in every celebration of the Mass?

Thank You, Jesus, for the blessing of being united with You in Holy Communion. I ask that I might receive fully the fruits of the Holy Mass I just participated in, so that I may live a happy and holy life following You.

Seventeenth Sunday in Ordinary Time

Longing for Jesus

⬡

Once, after a First Communion Mass, I attended a party for one of the children. The little girl told me how excited she was to receive Holy Communion each week.

The Prayer after Mass by St. Bonaventure speaks about desiring Jesus all the more (see today's prayer). With each reception of Holy Communion, our desire for Jesus should be all the greater. We see something similar in the Gospels, when Jesus multiplied the loaves of bread. The people who ate the miraculous bread had a greater hunger for the teachings of Jesus. Massive crowds followed Him, wanting to hear His words and witness His miraculous works.

When the public celebration of the Mass was suspended because of the COVID-19 pandemic, many of the Catholic faithful hungered for the Eucharist. When they were able to receive the Eucharist at Mass again, many were filled with tears. Others commented on how they missed Holy Communion and now were fulfilled once again by being united with Jesus in the Holy Eucharist.

Let us pray that with each Holy Communion, we will desire Jesus, who is the delight of our souls, all the more.

Meditations after Holy Communion

Points to Ponder

Each week, do you desire to receive the Eucharist?

If you miss Mass for some reason, do you notice a difference in your life, that something is missing? What do you most look forward to about Sunday Mass?

Do you ever notice the desires of your heart and soul for God? How has God fulfilled you throughout life?

Prayer after Mass
by St. Bonaventure

O sweetest Lord Jesus Christ, I implore Thee, pierce the very marrow of my soul with the delightful, health-giving dart of Thy love, with true, tranquil, holy, apostolic charity, so that my whole soul may ever languish and faint for love of Thee and for desire of Thee alone. May it long and pine for Thy courts; may it ever desire to be dissolved and to be with Thee. Grant that my soul may hunger for Thee, Who art the bread of angels, the comforting nourishment of all holy souls, our daily and most delectable bread, our supersubstantial bread, in which is found every sweet delight. May my heart ever hunger for Thee, on whom the angels lovingly gaze; may it feed on Thee; and may the innermost depths of my being be filled with the sweetness which comes from having tasted Thee. May my soul ever thirst for Thee, Who art the source of life, the fount of wisdom and knowledge, the brightness of everlasting light, the flood of all true happiness, the riches of the house of God.

May I at all times think of Thee; may I ever seek Thee and ever find Thee; may I always follow Thee and reach Thee; may Thy holy name be in my heart and on my lips; and to Thy praise and glory may every work of mine be done. Humble and discreet, loving and happy, ever ready and cheerful in Thy service, may I persevere, by Thy grace, even unto the end. Be Thou alone and evermore my hope; be Thou all my trust; be Thou my wealth, my delight, my joy, my consolation, my rest, my endless peace. Be Thou to me as a goodly taste, as a pleasant perfume, as a soothing sweetness. Be Thou my food and my refreshment; my refuge and my help; my wisdom; my portion, mine own possession and my treasure. In Thee, O Lord, may my mind and my heart remain fixed and firm, and rooted immovably for evermore. Amen.

A Powerful Moment with the Eucharist

One of the ways we continue our adoration of the Eucharistic Lord beyond Mass is through Eucharistic adoration. A consecrated Host is placed in a monstrance on the altar so that people may pray before the exposed presence of Jesus. Some people go to adoration once a week and spend an hour with Jesus. Other people might go when they have a big decision to make or when they are uncertain about what to do.

In 2008, I attended the International Eucharistic Congress in Canada with a group of young people. I was able to meet up with a friend of mine who is a religious sister, and her community was providing adorers for the adoration chapel. My friend told me that I should join her during her time slot for adoration — 3:00 a.m.! I didn't think I would go, but by God's grace, I woke up around that time and went to the adoration chapel. A sense of peace came over me as I sat there before the Blessed Sacrament and pondered where my life would take me. I had left the seminary and had no idea what to do with the rest of my life. Kneeling before the Eucharist, I knew that God had a plan for me.

Meditations after Holy Communion

At a different point in my life, when I felt crushed and defeated, I drove to an adoration chapel and asked Jesus for guidance as to what I should do. I poured out my heart to Him in that prayer time, and at the end of it, Jesus gave me comforting words in prayer.

Every encounter we have with the Eucharist, whether in Mass or in adoration, can be a powerful moment. Some moments might be more memorable than others. Pay attention to how you think Jesus might be speaking to you in the moment.

Points to Ponder

Have you ever had a powerful experience of the Eucharist that brought you peace or happiness in times of trial or sadness? Have you turned to Jesus in the Holy Eucharist at a difficult moment in your life? What happened?

Thank You, Jesus, for allowing me to receive You in Holy Communion. May my reception of Communion today, and every one going forward, be a powerful moment of grace and union with You.

Nineteenth Sunday in Ordinary Time

Do You Want Eternal Life?

In John's Gospel, chapter 6, Jesus gave a profound teaching about the Eucharist. It's popularly known as the Bread of Life discourse. In this passage, Jesus references the manna that fed the Israelites in the desert. He says that they ate the manna but still died. Jesus goes on to say that He is the Bread from Heaven and that whoever eats His Body and drinks His Blood will live forever. Jesus is the Bread come down from Heaven. He is the Son of God who comes to earth to redeem us from our sins. He instituted the Holy Eucharist on the night of the Last Supper when He said, "This is my Body.... This is my Blood." In the Bread of Life discourse, Jesus makes a bold promise to His hearers. But some of them are so turned off by this teaching that they turn away from Him and will no longer be counted as His followers.

When we hear this teaching of Jesus, it gives us hope in eternal life. Jesus promised that whoever eats His Body and drinks His Blood will live forever. Today at Mass, we did as Jesus asked by receiving Holy Communion, and now we continue to receive the promise of eternal life with God forever. Every time you come to Mass, remember that what you are doing and participating in brings life to your soul not only right now but for all eternity.

Points to Ponder

You might wish to read chapter 6 of John's Gospel and reflect on the teaching of Jesus. Do you believe that the Eucharist is an assurance of eternal life? Do you believe Jesus' teaching, or do you have doubts? If you had been there to hear the Bread of Life discourse, would you have kept following Jesus, or would you have walked away?

Jesus, thank You for coming to me in Holy Communion today. I know that because I eat Your Body and drink Your Blood, I have the promise of eternal life. Help me each day to live a life pleasing to You and worthy of the Kingdom of Heaven.

Twentieth Sunday in Ordinary Time

In Union with the Church
throughout the World

———————— ❀ ————————

Certain prayers use the language of universal union with the Church. In the Morning Offering, for instance, we pray, "O Jesus, through the Immaculate Heart of Mary, I offer You my prayers, works, joys, and sufferings of this day for all the intentions of Your Sacred Heart, in union with the Holy Sacrifice of the Mass throughout the world, in reparation for my sins, for the intentions of all my relatives and friends, and in particular for the intentions of the Holy Father. Amen." First thing in the morning, we can offer our day to God and ask for all the graces of the Holy Mass, by saying that we offer all of our prayers and works to Jesus in union with the Holy Sacrifice of the Mass.

The Pieta Prayer Book includes a "Prayer to Obtain the Grace of All the World's Masses." That is something to think about. Consider all the Masses that are celebrated throughout the world. It's quite possible that there is not a moment in the day when the Mass is not being celebrated. In all of these Masses, God is praised and pours out blessings and graces on the world. Every day, Mass is offered close to where you live. In larger cities, Masses abound throughout the morning hours, at noon, and in evening hours too.

This is the beauty of our Catholic Faith. No matter where we travel in the world, we are able to attend Mass and know what is happening, because it is the same Mass throughout the world. Bread and wine are consecrated into Jesus' Body and Blood, and we are blessed to receive the Holy Eucharist. The next time you attend Mass, pause for a moment and think how you are united with believers throughout the world who are experiencing and doing the same thing as you are. What a blessing! What a grace!

Points to Ponder

Do you know how many Masses are offered
in your area, and when? Have you ever
thought about going to daily Mass? What has
prevented you from attending daily Mass?

Pause to think about the Masses that are happening
throughout the world. They happen in war
zones; at shrines to Jesus, Mary, and the saints;
in foreign countries; and close to home. If there
was one place you could attend Mass, where
would it be? Have you ever prayed to receive
the graces of all the Masses of the world?

*Lord Jesus, thank You for allowing me to attend Mass
today and receive the precious gift of Your Body and
Blood in Holy Communion. I thank You for the priest*

who celebrated this Mass and for all the priests who are celebrating Mass throughout the world. I unite myself with believers throughout the world and offer my prayers and works in union with all the Masses celebrated in the world today. Allow me to receive the graces You wish to give me and always to be grateful for Your gifts.

Twenty-First Sunday in Ordinary Time

In Union with the Poor

Bishop Barron, in his popular series *Catholicism*, when talking about the Eucharist, referenced a story related to the mother of British historian Christopher Dawson. When Dawson sought to convert to Catholicism from Anglicanism, his mother said, "It's not the doctrine that concerns me. It's that now you will be worshipping with the help."

That's the beauty of gathering for Mass each Sunday. You might know many of the people there, especially if you are in a smaller community, but if you are in a larger community you might know only a fraction. The Mass draws people of all walks of life and all backgrounds. A person present at Mass might be a millionaire, a doctor, a blue-collar laborer, or someone who does not know where his next meal will come from. God calls all people to Mass—the rich and the poor, the sick and the healthy.

God calls us, as receivers of the Eucharist, to have a great concern for the poor. St. John Chrysostom said that we must see Christ in the beggar at the door of the church if we would see Him in the Eucharist we receive. When we come to Mass, we all, in a sense, become poor because we become beggars before the

Meditations after Holy Communion

God of the universe. Just as we receive many blessings from the Lord, as we are nourished by the Eucharist, He asks us to share those blessings with those who are less fortunate. The Eucharist we receive unites us to the poor and calls us to do what we can to help them in their need.

Points to Ponder

Do you know a poor person? What have been your experiences with the poor? Do you pass by the poor every day on your commute to work or in some other setting? When was the last time you supported the poor, the homeless, or the hungry? How might Jesus be calling you to serve them this week?

I am a poor beggar who is hungry for the Bread of Life. Thank you, Jesus, for feeding me today. As You have nourished me, show me how I can feed those who hunger today.

In Union with Those before You

Every church I enter, whether as the pastor of the parish or a guest, I stand in awe of the building that surrounds me. I marvel, for instance, at the beauty of the stained-glass windows. Typically, each window has a dedication or "in memoriam" of an individual or a group of people. When I sit down in the pew to pray or stand at the altar to say Mass, I think back to all the people who have worshipped in that place: the priests who stood there before me, the people who built the church, and those who have prayed there throughout the years; I even think of those who will come in the future. The church in which you just attended Mass exists because people worshipped there before you, gave of their resources, and helped the Church to continue her saving mission.

The reality of those who pray in a community became clear to me when I visited a local nursing home once for Mass. Due to my schedule, it had been a few months since I had said Mass there. There was a lady who was there every time I said Mass at the nursing home, and I had a memory of her from my early adult years when I would frequent a church in Green Bay for daily Mass. She was a daily Massgoer. I felt honored to be able to celebrate Mass and bring her the Eucharist in the nursing home. She wasn't one of my parishioners, so I didn't hear of her death. As I prepared for Mass that morning in the nursing home, I asked the residents where the lady with the oxygen was. I didn't know her name. They told me, sadly, that she had passed.

Remembering those who have worshipped before us gives them a certain proximity to us. As you attend Mass and receive the Eucharist, remember those who have gone before you in faith, who worshipped where you do and who, by their presence there, have given you the opportunity to receive the living God in that place.

Points to Ponder

Close your eyes and think of what your church must have been like years ago. Do you know of any people who worshipped there long ago? If you can, call to mind someone you know who has passed away, how that person's spot is now empty, and how his or her absence from the Church visible is known to us.

Thank You, Jesus, for those who have come to this place of worship before me. Thank You for their dedication so I can now be here and receive You in Holy Communion. Grant them eternal rest and a place at the banquet table in the Kingdom of Heaven.

Twenty-Third Sunday in Ordinary Time

A Heart-to-Heart with Jesus

The English Anglican convert to Catholicism St. John Henry Cardinal Newman had the motto *Cor ad cor loquitur*, which means "heart speaks to heart." Throughout this book, I wish to encourage us to pause every few weeks and have that heart-to-heart with Jesus. This is a method of prayer in which we can relate to Jesus all of our emotions, whether fear, anger, loneliness, sadness, joy, or whatever they might be. All too often, we rely on scripted prayer, memorized prayer, or rote prayer, but in a healthy spiritual life, we need to dialogue with Jesus using our own words and have spontaneous prayer. An apropos time comes to us every weekend after receiving Holy Communion. This book seeks to be a training for such casual conversation: pondering the points each week and answering the questions is a way in which you can begin to dialogue with God.

Cor ad cor loquitur, heart speaks to heart. Let your heart speak to Jesus, and His Heart, which beats out of love for you, will speak to you — most likely inaudibly (on rare occasions, audibly). Over time, as you allow your heart to speak to His, you will know when His heart is speaking to yours.

Meditations after Holy Communion

Points to Ponder

Have a heart-to-heart with Jesus. What is on
your mind? What are your fears? Your joys?
Your sorrows? Don't leave anything unsaid.

*Thank You, Jesus, for allowing me to receive You in
Holy Communion and to spend these moments with
You in silent prayer. Thank You for listening to my fears
and joys. I know You hear me, and I know You speak
to me. Open the ear of my heart, that I may hear Your
Heart speaking to mine, not only on this day, but every
day of my life.*

Twenty-Fourth Sunday in Ordinary Time

A Pledge of Love and Service

One of my friends created an audio Bible, and he jokes with me that at the end of Mass, when we are told to "go and announce the Gospel of the Lord," he says, "I do" in virtue of the audio Bible. Other dismissals tell us, "Go forth" or "Go in peace, glorifying the Lord by your life." These are the marching orders given to us by God as we go forth filled with God's presence, love, and grace from the Mass celebrated and the Eucharist received.

Our reception of Holy Communion becomes a pledge of our love and service to Almighty God because the God who St. John tells us is love becomes a part of us. Filled with God's love, we can do nothing in return but love Him, serve Him, and make Him known. In Matthew, chapter 25, Jesus tells us that He is present in the poor—that when we feed them, clothe them, visit them, and so forth, we do these things for Him. We glorify God by our lives when we serve and love our neighbor. Every Sunday, we hear the Gospel of Jesus proclaimed, and then we hear a homily on the Scripture readings. This is the Gospel we are to announce not only by words but by how we live our lives. As you are sent forth from Mass by Christ's mandate in the Gospel to go and make disciples, you do so by loving and serving God and neighbor.

Points to Ponder

To whom do you think Jesus is sending you this week? Have you ever asked Jesus to send you to serve whomever He wants you to serve?

In what ways do you already glorify God by your life?

If you are to announce the gospel, what part of the gospel do you announce? How have you announced the gospel in the past? How do you think you will announce the gospel this week?

What does it mean to go in peace? Do you possess peace? Do you exude and share peace with others?

Thank You, Jesus, for filling me with Your love through the Eucharist I have received. I pledge my life to You and wish to love You above all things. I ask that my love for You will overflow to all I meet this week as I glorify You by my life and announce Your gospel.

Twenty-Fifth Sunday in Ordinary Time

Invited to the Feast

"Come to the feast of Heaven and Earth, come to the table of plenty." This line from the popular song "Table of Plenty" indicates an invitation. God invites us to Sunday Mass every week. But like any other invitation we receive, we have a choice in the matter: we can either go, or we can ignore it. Our lives are busy. They are filled with many activities. Many of us are overscheduled. It is very easy to say that we don't have time for Mass or that we want to use that one to two hours for something else.

The celebration of Mass is a heavenly invitation. We are invited to the wedding feast of the Lamb. The Mass is a participation in the heavenly liturgy as we join the angels and saints in their song of praise. There is no other invitation or task that can compare to what Jesus offers us each week—complete union with Him through our reception of Holy Communion. Today you said yes to Jesus' invitation. He said, "I want to make my home with you today." And by your amen when you received Communion, you have allowed that to happen. Pray for the grace never to say no to that invitation.

Meditations after Holy Communion

Points to Ponder

What are some of the reasons you have chosen not to
attend Mass in the past? Are there any valid reasons,
besides illness or pandemics or some emergency,
for us to say no to God's heavenly invitation?

Are there people in your family or among your
friends who should go to Mass but do not?
Who are they? God invited you to Mass; whom
could you invite to church next week?

*Thank You, Jesus, for inviting me to the supper of the
Lamb to feast on your Body and Blood. You invite me
week in and week out. I want to say yes every week,
but sometimes it is difficult. Please remove all the
obstacles that get in the way of Sunday Mass so that
I will always say yes to the graces You offer me each
Sunday.*

Twenty-Sixth Sunday in Ordinary Time

Asking for Forgiveness

"Brothers and sisters, let us call to mind our sins, and so prepare ourselves to celebrate the sacred mysteries." This is how we begin each and every Mass. It makes us aware that we are sinners in need of God's mercy and forgiveness. During that brief pause, do you call to mind a sin or two and ask for forgiveness? During the Our Father, which we pray not only during Mass but also at other times throughout the day, we ask God to forgive our trespasses. Later in the Mass, we ask Jesus, as the Lamb of God, to take away the sins of the world and once again beg Him for mercy. The Mass is filled with opportunities to ask for God's mercy and forgiveness. In fact, the Eucharist we receive remits venial sins. The Eucharist becomes a way in which we experience forgiveness, unworthy as we are.

The Eucharist is a powerful aid against sin in our lives. Many saints have been drawn out of the depths of despair and hopelessness by daily reception of the Eucharist. An addict can be set free by the grace of the sacrament. It is truly astonishing what God can do through the graces of the Eucharist. Whatever struggle you are facing right now, receiving Holy Communion can strengthen you in your battle and make firm your resolve.

Meditations after Holy Communion

Points to Ponder

Is there a sin in your life that you are aware of
that you would like to address? How can the
Eucharist help you to fight that sin? How has the
Eucharist already helped you grow in virtue?

*Lord Jesus, thank You for allowing me to receive You
in the Eucharist today and for the forgiveness You have
extended to me. I need Your help every day. By the
power of the Eucharist and the graces You offer me,
help me to overcome the sins in my life that separate me
from You.*

Mary's First Reception of Holy Communion

Jesus instituted the Eucharist at the Last Supper, and when He said, "Do this in memory of me," He commanded the apostles to continue to celebrate what they experienced. We know that the early Church gathered for the celebration of the Mass and that the apostles perpetuated the Last Supper. Mary, the Mother of Jesus, lived in close proximity to the apostles, especially John, to whose care Jesus entrusted her. It should be no stretch of the imagination for us to think about Mary receiving her First Holy Communion and receiving the Eucharist throughout her life. Stained-glass windows and paintings depict this. One has only to think of the Dahlgren Chapel at Georgetown University or the Poor Clare Colletine convent in Rockford, Illinois.

Fr. Daniel Lord, the author who inspired this book of Eucharistic meditations, reflected on Mary's First Holy Communion in his book *Song of the Rosary*, in which he imagines Mary cleaning the Upper Room and eating a crumb off the plate or sipping the last drop from the chalice. It could be true. Or is it Fr. Lord's pious imagination? Nonetheless, at some point, Mary did receive the Eucharist for the first time. What must that have been like?

Meditations after Holy Communion

Points to Ponder

What do you think it was like for Mary to receive
her First Holy Communion? After the Ascension,
it was through the Eucharist that she could once
again have union with her Son. As she sat in the
congregation when the apostles offered the Eucharist,
what went through her mind? Spend a few moments
contemplating the thoughts and actions of Mary.

*Jesus, I wish to be united to You as Your Mother was in
this life, for she received You into her very body through
the Incarnation and then the Eucharist. As I receive the
Eucharist today, allow her prayer to become my prayer
and her union with You to become mine.*

Twenty-Eighth Sunday in Ordinary Time

Mary's Last Communion

Two mystical biographies of Mary, one by Venerable Mary of Agreda and the other by Blessed Anne Catherine Emmerich, provide accounts of Mary's receiving Holy Communion on her deathbed, similar to our idea of Viaticum today. Whether this took place or not, and even though it is outside of Scripture, we may give it some consideration.

In some accounts of the end of Mary's life, the apostles all gathered at her bedside, beckoned from all corners of the earth to be with the Queen of Apostles in her last days. It was prior to her falling asleep or passing from this world that she received the Holy Eucharist for the last time. As the apostles celebrated the Eucharist, she received Holy Communion and shared communion with her Son. This act of final communion for Mary meant that she would be reunited with her Son very soon. Her last reception foreshadowed the final reunification of a Mother and Son.

Meditations after Holy Communion

Points to Ponder

Reflect on the question of Mary's last days. Do you think she died a death like her Son, or was she assumed body and soul while still alive? Regardless of whether she died, Mary did receive the Eucharist one last time in her life. Ponder that moment as she awaited her final reunification with Christ in Heaven.

Jesus, You have taken Your Mother to be with You, body and soul, in eternal life. As I have received Holy Communion today, I am united with You sacramentally, and I look forward to being united with You for all eternity in Heaven.

Twenty-Ninth Sunday in Ordinary Time

Behold the Lamb!

———— ✦ ————

Before we all receive Holy Communion, the priest invites us, "Behold the Lamb of God, behold Him who takes away the sins of the world. Blessed are those called to the supper of the Lamb." "Behold" is a command. It means to stop what you are doing, stop thinking about worldly things, stop the wandering eye, and look forward and see Jesus before you. Behold. Pause. Gaze. Wonder. Contemplate. These are all things we can do in that moment of beholding.

Think of a mother who beholds her newborn infant. Picture her glance of love she has for the child. This is how we are to approach the mystery of the Eucharist. We behold a great mystery: that God who was invisible became visible, through the Incarnation, in Jesus Christ. Jesus then took bread, blessed and broke it, and gave it to His disciples, saying, "This is my Body." And now we behold this reality: that what appears to be ordinary bread is actually the Body of Christ. We cannot grasp such a reality. We cannot fathom it. That is why we behold.

John the Baptist pointed out Jesus to his followers, saying, "Behold the Lamb of God" (John 1:29). John wanted them to know Jesus and to follow Him. Now we hear those words, wanting to know Jesus more and desiring to be better followers of Him.

Points to Ponder

Spend a few minutes beholding the Lamb through the Scriptures — before the manger in Bethlehem, at the foot of the Cross, after the Resurrection. Behold the reality of Jesus, who came to live among us, to heal us, to teach us, and to save us from our sins.

Lord Jesus, in this moment after Holy Communion, I pause to behold Your greatness. Teach me this week how I can continue to behold all the ways You manifest Your power and greatness in my life and in the world.

For the Holy Souls

During the Universal Prayer (the Prayer of the Faithful), one of the final petitions is usually for the intention of the Mass. You might be familiar with this Catholic practice by which you can have a Mass said for an intention for a small stipend, usually ten dollars. Think of the stipend as a contribution for the day's liturgy — heat, electricity, candles, and so forth. The intention is usually for the deceased, but it is also common to have Masses celebrated for the living, whether for someone's intentions or for his or her health. Every weekend, a Mass is offered "For the People," meaning for all the living and deceased members of the parish.

The idea of having a Mass said for a loved one who has died is to assist that person on his or her journey to the Kingdom of Heaven. Should the person's soul be detained in Purgatory, the grace of the Mass aids in his or her purification. According to St. Thomas Aquinas, if a soul for whom a Mass is offered already enjoys eternal bliss in Heaven, the soul experiences an increase in accidental glory, that is, the efficacy of that person's intercession for his or her loved ones on earth.

Meditations after Holy Communion

When we have Masses said for loved ones and friends who have died, it is a way for us to continue to share in life with them. From their place in eternity, they are able to participate. A First Communion Mass I celebrated was offered for the father of one of the students; he had passed away a few years earlier from cancer. Even though this dad could not be physically present, he was remembered and prayed for and was able to participate from beyond the grave.

When you attend Mass, it can be a time for you to connect with your loved ones. Maybe a hymn that is sung reminds you of them, or you feel close to them for some reason. At every Mass, you, as a member of the praying community, can bring your intention. "Pray, brothers and sisters that my sacrifice and yours may be acceptable to God, the almighty Father." You participate in the priest's sacrifice and can offer it for your intention. When you want to feel close to someone who has passed away, remember that person at Mass, and experience a spiritual closeness to him or her.

Points to Ponder

Whom do you want to remember at Mass? Have you felt the closeness of a deceased loved one at Mass or at another time in your life?

Thank You, Jesus, for allowing me to receive You in Holy Communion today. I ask that, as I am united to Heaven through the sacrifice of the Mass, N. (name the person) may receive graces from my sacrificial offering. I wish to be close to N. May eternal rest and perpetual light be N's.

Thirty-First Sunday in Ordinary Time

Thanksgiving

During every Mass, at the Consecration, before the priest repeats the words of Jesus at the Last Supper, he introduces those words with these: "Jesus took bread, gave thanks, broke it, and gave it to the disciples." Another common expression for the Mass is "the celebration the Eucharist." The word "Eucharist" means "thanksgiving." Each time we celebrate Mass, it is an occasion for us to give thanks.

There are many things for which we could thank God. For instance, we can thank Him for the personal blessings He has bestowed upon us or for the gift of life. Of course, this book is about making a Eucharistic thanksgiving, meaning that we give thanks to God for the opportunity of receiving the Body and Blood of Jesus in Holy Communion.

In the United States, we gather with our families on the fourth Thursday of November, and together we break bread and share a meal, much like what Jesus did with His disciples at the Last Supper. On that day, our entire country gives thanks for what we have received. Our secular Thanksgiving comes but once a year. Our religious thanksgiving happens every time we celebrate

Mass and receive the Eucharist. The next time you go to Mass, consider it your weekly Thanksgiving Day.

Points to Ponder

Consider all the things in your life for which you are grateful: the gift of life; your parents; your family; the many blessings you have received. Then consider the ways God has guided your life. Be sure to express your thanksgiving.

Lord Jesus, thank You for the many blessings with which You have filled my life, but most especially for the gift of receiving You in Holy Communion today and every time I come to Mass.

Thirty-Second Sunday in Ordinary Time

Your Last Communion

I have never had the opportunity to say Mass for the Missionaries of Charity, the religious community founded by St. Teresa of Calcutta, but I am told by those who have that in the sacristy there is a sign for the priest to see as he vests. The sign says this: "Priest of God, celebrate this Mass as if it was your first Mass, your last Mass, your only Mass." It is a stark reminder to the priest to remember what it is he is doing and whom it is he serves and offers to the people of God. In another sense, it has a "memento mori" feeling to it. On Catholic social media, the hashtag #MementoMori was popularized by Daughter of St. Paul Sr. Theresa Aletheia Noble. The idea behind the phrase and movement is to remember daily your death. Doing this is an invitation for us to live our best and holiest lives possible, realizing that today is a gift and tomorrow is not guaranteed.

The last weeks of Ordinary Time focus on the Last Things and help us call to mind, each year, that one day we will die. This reality might have hit home with you with the news of someone's unexpected death, which takes a person by surprise. As a priest, one week I gave Communion to a gentleman who sat in the back of church, and the next week I celebrated his funeral. I had not known the previous Sunday that I was giving him his last Communion, which became his food and strength for the journey home to God after a stroke. One day, death will come for us, and the Eucharist we celebrate and receive prepares us for that day. What if today's Communion were your last?

Points to Ponder

If today were your last day on earth, would you
be satisfied with the life you lived? Are you at
peace with God? Wrestle with the fact that
this could be the last Communion you receive,
because we do not know the day or the hour of the
Lord's coming or when He will call us home.

*Lord Jesus, help me to cherish my reception of the
Eucharist today as if it were the last time I received
You on earth, before being completely united to You in
eternal life.*

Thirty-Third Sunday in Ordinary Time

Send Us Your Angels

The angels are all around us. Jesus teaches in the Gospel that each of us has a guardian angel. In Scripture, we meet some of the archangels: Raphael, Gabriel, and Michael. And at some Catholic churches you attend, there's a good chance that you pray the St. Michael Prayer at the conclusion of Mass. Pope Leo XIII had a vision of the terror and reign of Satan, and St. Michael waged battle against the evil forces. It was this vision that prompted Pope Leo XIII to pen the St. Michael Prayer. The prayer we all know is the abridged version; the original prayer is much longer.

As the liturgical year comes to a close and a new one begins with the First Sunday of Advent, the Church's liturgy focuses on the presence of angels. Angels play an important role in the Mass. When I was a young boy serving Mass, the pious lady sacristan at the church wanted to teach me about the Faith and the importance of serving at the altar. One day, she commented that at every Mass, especially during the Eucharistic Prayer, when we all kneel, the angels are present and surrounding the altar. To this very day, as I stand at the altar and celebrate Mass as a priest, I call to mind what that woman told the young Eddie, who now stands *in persona Christi,* saying the words of consecration and surrounded by the angels.

Today let us ask God to send us His angels to help us during our pilgrimage to the Kingdom of Heaven, so that we may spend all eternity with the angels, praising and worshipping Almighty God.

Points to Ponder

How often do you pray to your guardian angel? Do you live with an awareness of the invisible realities — that is to say, the forces of good and evil — that surround you?

What images of the angels do you have in your mind? What do you know about the angels?

Lord Jesus, Your coming as man was announced by an angel, and Your return in glory will be ushered in by angels. Through the Holy Eucharist I receive, make me aware of these spiritual realities. With Your sacramental grace and the help of St. Michael and my guardian angel, may I fend off evil and desire to follow You all the days of my life.

Jesus Christ, King of the Universe

An Audience with the King

Have you ever met a famous person? If you had the opportunity to converse with a famous person, what would you say to him or her? Maybe you have been privileged to have a conversation with a president, a star, an athlete, or some other dignitary. When people think back on such experiences, they sometimes say, "I wish I would have said this" or "I wish I would have told them that." We might even experience those thoughts about a person we know who died and we think of our last conversation with him or her. I think back to the last phone call I had with my mother, and if I had known it would be my last, I would have talked longer.

When someone meets the pope, we say that the person had an audience with the pope. At every Mass, there is an opportunity for us to have an audience with a King: Jesus, who is King of Kings and Lord of Lords. The audience begins as soon as we enter the church and kneel in our pew in prayer before the tabernacle. The King speaks to us in the Scriptures we hear. And the King visits us as we approach to receive Him in Holy Communion. Our audience continues when we go back to the pew and kneel down again. In that moment, we talk to the King and share all that is on our minds and hearts. The best thing is, when we leave church, if there's something we forgot to tell Him, we can do so in that moment, and we can express it the next time we have that intimate audience at the next Mass. In our special audience with the King of the Universe, not only do we talk, but we listen to the One who offers the greatest counsel possible.

Points to Ponder

Have you had conversations with people and wished you had said something that you forgot or didn't think to say at the time? Did you ever get the opportunity to share that thought?

If you could ask Jesus anything, what would it be? How did Jesus speak to you today at Mass? What is it that you want to tell the King today?

Thank You, Jesus, for listening to me and for the words You speak to me. You bless me with Your Eucharistic presence in every Holy Communion. What am I to say to You, except that I love You, adore You, thank You, and praise You.

Other Holy Days

Assumption of the Blessed Virgin Mary (August 15)

Let Me Live in Your Presence One Day

The Responsorial Psalm for the solemnity of the Assumption acclaims, "The queen stands at your right hand, arrayed in gold" (see Ps. 45:9). Mary as the Queen Mother takes her place in Heaven through the Assumption and stands at God's right hand as an advocate and intercessor for the Christian people. What we celebrate on the solemnity of the Assumption is God's bringing Mary's body and soul into Heaven. What God does for Mary He one day will do for all of us in the final resurrection of the body. After Jesus ascended into Heaven, certainly Mary longed for the day when she would be with her Son again. She lived every day longing to live in the presence of Christ.

The Gospel for the Assumption recounts the visit of Mary to Elizabeth and the infant John's leaping in the womb of Elizabeth. John found himself in the presence of Jesus and was filled with joy for the Lord. We come in contact with Jesus, reserved in the tabernacle in the church or exposed in a monstrance (often in an adoration chapel). What we experience here on earth by being in the presence of the Eucharistic Lord is only a foretaste of what living in His presence forever with Mary and all the saints will be like. On this feast of the Assumption, as we remember Jesus bringing His Mother, Mary, into Heaven, we pray to be filled with the longing to live in His presence not only when we can in this life, but for all eternity.

Points to Ponder

How often do you find time to be in the presence of Jesus? Do you live your life desiring to live in God's presence forever in Heaven? How could you deepen your desire for God's presence? How could you become more aware of God's presence in your life?

Thank You, Jesus, for allowing me to be in Your presence today. With every Holy Communion, I pray for the grace to desire to live with You for all eternity.

All Saints' Day (November 1)

In Communion with the Saints

Have you ever thought about the great treasure we have in our Catholic Faith? I often marvel at our rich history, knowing that God has called so many men and women to great degrees of holiness. The example of the saints encourages me to strive for holiness. Every now and again, I find myself thinking about some of my favorite saints and what their lives must have been like. One day, as I was sitting in church before the Blessed Sacrament, I couldn't help but marvel at the many priest saints. St. John Vianney immediately came to mind—probably because he would also pray before the tabernacle in his church. This led me to wonder what his prayer life consisted of. How did he pray for his parishioners?

A similar thought struck me as I reflected after Mass one day. I considered the fact that as I received Holy Communion that day, many other saints had that privilege too. And I sat mulling over what that must have been like for them, St. Thérèse of Lisieux came to mind. I recalled her visit to Our Lady of Victories, a parish church in Paris, and also her trip to Rome to see the Holy Father and seek permission to enter Carmel at an early age. Surely Thérèse received Holy Communion during those travels; that provided another subject for my meditation. What was it like for a saint to receive Holy Communion? How did the Eucharist sustain her? Did it give her strength? How did she pray? Thinking about those questions brought my level of prayer after Holy Communion to higher levels.

Points to Ponder

Which saint do you admire the most? Do any quotations from them or memories of their experiences found in their writings come to mind? If so, allow that to guide your personal meditation. If not, imagine the saint kneeling right next to you. What do you see? Do you hear anything?

Jesus, make me a saint. Give me the desire to love You as Your saints did and to live my life based on their example.

Immaculate Conception (December 8)

God Has Chosen Me

The feast of the Immaculate Conception recalls God's saving work in history and, in a singular way, in the life of Mary. Due to the Fall of Adam and Eve, the wrong in the world had to be put right again, and this was to be accomplished by the death of Jesus on the Cross. By the grace of the Cross, the original disobedience was corrected by the obedience of Jesus, who died willingly for sinners. The ancient tree that brought about the curse of sin was corrected by the tree of life, on which hung the Savior of the world.

In the order of time, the Father sent His son, Jesus, to become incarnate of the Virgin Mary. God chose Mary for this special task, to which she assented when she gave her *fiat*—that is, "let it be done to me"—during the angel Gabriel's visit to her home in Nazareth. Because God chose Mary for this special role in salvation history, the solemnity of the Immaculate Conception remembers God's saving action in the life of Mary from the very moment of her conception. God foresaw the merits of the Cross and applied the graces of redemption to Mary before the action occurred in history, thereby preserving her from the taint of Original Sin and allowing her to be free from sin throughout her life.

God chose Mary for a special mission in history. He has chosen you and me for a special mission too. Through holy Baptism, the Original Sin in us was wiped away, and we were claimed for Christ Jesus by the sign of the Cross and called into mission as disciples of Jesus. God chose you. Mary discovered her calling by Gabriel's announcement. We discover our calling by following God's voice deep within us. One way we can discern how God chose us is to be still after receiving Holy Communion, knowing that God is within us and wants to speak to us in that moment.

Points to Ponder

God preserved Mary from all sin. What sin do you wish Jesus would take away from your life?

God chose Mary to be the Mother of Jesus. Can you trace how God called you at particular moments in your life for a special purpose? What was God's calling for you last week? How did you rise to the occasion?

How is God calling you, choosing you, directing you right now? Spend a few moments in silence and be attentive to how God is working deep within you.

Thank You, Jesus, for choosing me to be Your disciple and to be Your follower. I wish to follow Your call for my life in all that I do. Help me, strengthened by the Eucharist I have received, to remain faithful to You and the way You have chosen me to serve in the world.

About the Author

Fr. Edward Looney was ordained a priest for the Diocese of Green Bay in June 2015 and is an internationally recognized Marian theologian, writer, speaker, and radio personality. He is a member of the Mariological Society of America and since 2016 has served on their administrative council. In 2020, he was elected vice president of the society. He is the best-selling author of *A Heart Like Mary's* (Ave Maria Press), *A Rosary Litany* (Our Sunday Visitor), *Our Lady of Good Help: A Prayer Book for Pilgrims* (TAN Books), and *A Lenten Journey with Mother Mary* (Sophia Institute Press). His writings appear in many print publications and online at *Catholic Exchange* and Aleteia. He also hosts the podcast *How They Love Mary*. Fr. Looney serves two rural Wisconsin parishes. You can follow him on social media at @FrEdwardLooney.

Sophia Institute

Sophia Institute is a nonprofit institution that seeks to nurture the spiritual, moral, and cultural life of souls and to spread the Gospel of Christ in conformity with the authentic teachings of the Roman Catholic Church.

Sophia Institute Press fulfills this mission by offering translations, reprints, and new publications that afford readers a rich source of the enduring wisdom of mankind.

Sophia Institute also operates the popular online resource CatholicExchange.com. *Catholic Exchange* provides world news from a Catholic perspective as well as daily devotionals and articles that will help readers to grow in holiness and live a life consistent with the teachings of the Church.

In 2013, Sophia Institute launched Sophia Institute for Teachers to renew and rebuild Catholic culture through service to Catholic education. With the goal of nurturing the spiritual, moral, and cultural life of souls, and an abiding respect for the role and work of teachers, we strive to provide materials and programs that are at once enlightening to the mind and ennobling to the heart; faithful and complete, as well as useful and practical.

Sophia Institute gratefully recognizes the Solidarity Association for preserving and encouraging the growth of our apostolate over the course of many years. Without their generous and timely support, this book would not be in your hands.

www.SophiaInstitute.com
www.CatholicExchange.com
www.SophiaInstituteforTeachers.org

Sophia Institute Press® is a registered trademark of Sophia Institute.
Sophia Institute is a tax-exempt institution as defined by the
Internal Revenue Code, Section 501(c)(3). Tax ID 22-2548708.